IMAGES
of America

CASHMERE

IMAGES
of America

CASHMERE

L. Burton Brender with the
Cashmere Museum & Pioneer Village
Foreword by Ray Schmitten
Afterword by Alexandra R. Palmer-Gapper

ARCADIA
PUBLISHING

Published by Arcadia Publishing
Charleston, South Carolina

Printed in the United States of America

Library of Congress Control Number: 2019931286

For all general information, please contact Arcadia Publishing:
Telephone 843-853-2070
Fax 843-853-0044
E-mail sales@arcadiapublishing.com
For customer service and orders:
Toll-Free 1-888-313-2665

Visit us on the Internet at www.arcadiapublishing.com

*For my father, who gave me my hometown; my mother,
who taught me to love it; my brothers, who grew up
Cashmere; and my children, to whom I pass it on.*

CONTENTS

FOREWORD

Cashmere is my home, and I echo more than a century of my family who have been able to say that. In 1902, my ancestor F.W. Schmitten brought his young family to Brender Canyon with a team of draft horses. He settled on a small piece of land in the beauty of the foothills, felling trees for lumber from his open-walled sawmill. But beauty, as they say, is only skin deep.

The people of this valley, not its scenery, are what make it incredible. The roots of the farmers here go as deep as the pear trees that they nurture, and the dreams of the new generation—well, they reach as high as the pines.

I have always called Cashmere my own, as did my father, my grandfather, and my great-grandfather. I feel I have something here, or perhaps something about it has me. The unchanging silhouette of the mountains, the variety of the four seasons, and the depth of community keep me.

The history of Cashmere echoes with memories of friends and family in my mind. I cannot help it, the hills themselves are daily reminders of times and people I love. My grandfather's playmates jumping off "Big Rock" into the swift Wenatchee. My father's friends hiking up the slopes covered with winter snow to ski into their fathers' orchards. The return of my generation from our country's wars, renewing their lives and having children of their own.

As for my family, 75 years of our daily life began and ended with a mill whistle. With time comes change, though, and today my kids return to school amid the constant din of fruit trucks delivering the valley's apples and pears to storage. Yet, like my forefathers, the Wenatchee River still draws us in on those hot August days, the mountains call when the fresh powder of January falls, and our children return to start their own new generation as fruit trucks roll home.

For me, for my family, Cashmere is special. A wonderful place to live, a wonderful place to grow up—and a wonderful place to call home.

—Ray Schmitten
August 6, 2018
Cashmere, Washington

ACKNOWLEDGMENTS

No book of history is a solitary work. While there are many people who helped me to create *Cashmere*, there are a few who stand out. Foremost among these are Alexandra R. "Lexie" Palmer-Gapper, director of the Cashmere Museum & Pioneer Village; Fred Harvey, curator of the Cashmere Museum & Pioneer Village; and retired junior high youth pastor Joseph Brouillette, Christ Center. Their depth of knowledge and sheer patience were absolutely instrumental to this research.

Also key were Congregational Care pastor Joyce Williams, Christ Center, for her primary documents and coordination within the ecumenical community, and senior pastor Steve Haney, Christ Center, for his emphatic encouragement. Many thanks are also due to orchardist Ray Schmitten for his foreword; the aforementioned Lexie for her afterword; retired Cashmere postmaster Linda Ingraham, now of the Cashmere American Legion, for her selfless dedication to local history and civic duty; Andrew Wilson of the Institute of Heraldry for his artistry; Melanie Wachholder, curator of collections, Wenatchee Valley Museum and Cultural Center, for her wonderful pictures (and demeanor); and pastor Charles Clarke, Cashmere Presbyterian Church, for his congregational history. In addition, I particularly want to thank Elizabeth Brender for her constant good advice and patient insight, Shelly Meier for her steadfast love, and my fellow historians and cousins Dick Brender and Garth Brender and their compatriot Tom Hart, who tirelessly championed the digitization of the *Cashmere Valley Record* (a publication to which I am unspeakably indebted).

I am additionally thankful for all of the talented and dedicated authors of the Olympia Writers Group and my "beta readers" Rick Taylor, Mark Teply, Leslie Roemer, Tiffany Grassman, Fred Harvey, Sarah Coutts, Laura Jordan, and the retired Colville language researcher Ernest K'saw's Brooks, who were the first to hear all about Cashmere. And, though I did not have the honor of meeting with most of the following scholars personally, I owe a debt of gratitude to each for their deep knowledge of language, the Greater Wenatchee Valley, and the Wenatchi people: Dr. Ewa Czaykowska-Higgins of the University of British Columbia; Dr. Andrew McKenzie of the University of Kansas; the late Dr. M. Dale Kinkade, also of the University of Kansas (and a graduate of the former Peshastin-Dryden High School); Richard Scheuerman; John Clement; and Dr. Nancy Mattina of the University of Montana.

Lastly, I want to thank Erin Vosgien and Angel Hisnanick at Arcadia Publishing for seeing a young writer through this process—you guys are *skookum*! Each of these people and many, many more, gave their time, money, and special attention for this book to come to print. Thank you.

Unless otherwise noted, all photographs are courtesy of the Cashmere Museum & Pioneer Village. All errors and omissions are my own.

INTRODUCTION

Cashmere, the center of Washington State, is unique. Of course, I am certain that there are other cities that one could say that about. There are certainly many small places in America that are orchard towns, or that are set in mountain foothills, or that were founded on faith and a belief in the decency of man. But none, I think, weave them together as beautifully as Cashmere, my hometown.

Many years ago, my middle school science teacher Jeff Kenoyer taught my class that the foothills of the Cascade Mountains, in which Cashmere lies, were the result of the great Missoula Floods. These monstrous torrents deluged the eastern half of the Pacific Northwest at the end of the last ice age. They were so big, he said, that the 800-foot hills surrounding the town were in part the creation of the flowing waters, which shaped them like ripples in a titanic stream. After the flood, the ironically sparse rain that came over the Cascades from Puget Sound wore the edges of these giant waves of earth smooth and nourished the desert-suited sage that grew there. Below in the valley, the Wenatchee River ran from its headwaters in the Cascades to its confluence with the Columbia 10 miles downstream.

According to historian Laura Arksey of HistoryLink, the P'squosa were the first known humans to settle Nt'wt'c'kum, the "Soaking Place," the area that would later become Cashmere. The P'squosa, perhaps better known as the Wenatchi, tell that the Creator Haw'iyuncútun first made the earth without humans, and for many years the Animal People ruled it. The Wolf, Salmon, Bear, Blue Jay, and many others thrived on the land and in the waters under the leadership of the wise and cagey Chief Coyote. Yet the Animal People knew that eventually Man would come, because the Creator had foretold it.

As recounted by Elle E. Clark in *Indian Legends of the Pacific Northwest*, the world waited many ages under the Animal People before the Creator fulfilled his prophecy. One day, a monstrous spirit in the form of a giant beaver descended upon Lake Cle Elum, a body of water just north of modern-day Roslyn, Washington. Chief Coyote, in defense of the Animal People, met the murderous beast in single combat. Fighting with all of their strength, Coyote and the monster struggled, carving a channel through the land that soon filled with water to become the Columbia River. The battle lasted for days and there were many times Chief Coyote feared for his life. Finally, though, at the edge of the Pacific Ocean, Coyote gained the upper hand and slew his foe, chopping its body into pieces. Flinging the parts in different directions, he gave them each a name and a prophecy. Upon touching the earth, the remains of his enemy became the different tribes of Indians, each bearing the name and identity that Chief Coyote gave them.

According to Richard Scheurman's *The Wenatchee Valley: And its First Peoples*, the 19th-century Upper Yakama leader Owhi once said "God was before the earth, the heavens were clear and good, and all things in the heavens were good. God looked one way then the other and named our lands for us to take care of." The Indians spread out and made their homes on the good earth east of the ocean. Though some resisted their arrival, like the evil Owl Sisters, whom Haw'iyuncútun executed, the Animal People soon welcomed Man as their brothers and sisters and together they thrived in nature's balance of give and take. Even today, many deeply spiritual Columbia Plateau Indians, of whom the P'squosa are one, live out these beliefs in pursuit of harmony and a righteous life.

The P'squosa lived off of the land, often foraging for the small, bulb-like root camas, a staple of their diet. They combined this starchy vegetable and other local plants with salmon from the Wenatchee River and wild game. They were a semi-nomadic people, migrating throughout the year between their sacred winter fishery in Winátsa (Tumwater Canyon in modern-day Leavenworth) to the milder Nt'wt'c'kum in the summer. When sedentary, they lived in wooden pit houses and tule huts, structures made of a native, reed-like plant.

The P'squosa spoke nxaʔamxcín (en-ha'am-ha-cheen), what modern linguists like Ewa Czaykowska-Higgins and the late M. Dale Kinkade call Moses-Columbia. This language is a form of Interior Salish closely related to that of other plateau peoples east of the mountains, and akin, albeit more distantly, to the speech of the coastal Pacific Northwest Native Americans. Trade between Salish speakers was common, and the P'squosa did not frequently war within their language family. They were never very populous, and anthropologists estimate that they never exceeded a few thousand at any one time. Yet even this small number has since dwindled, and the linguistics research group Ethnologue estimated in 2010 that only 17 living Moses-Columbia speakers were still alive. Indeed, when I was researching the language in 2016, I found only three. Since contact with Europeans, though, pieces of the P'squosa's language have passed into the regional speech of the Americans who settled the area. Salish words like skookum, meaning "big" or "good"; hi-yup, which translates roughly to "good friend"; and -chuck, a suffix that denotes a stream, are still in more or less common use.

Europeans appeared in the Pacific Northwest in the late 18th century, beginning the inexorable encroachment of foreign influence. By the mid-19th century, American military envoys made official contact with the Wenatchi, and soon thereafter the leading edge of American culture came to the valley. By the beginning of the 20th century, English had replaced nxaʔamxcín, the Wenatchis' native tongue, as the area's dominant language.

Still, the valley was not a place of violent struggle, and I think that is another thing that makes it unique. Though there was great sickness amid the native population after contact, there are no records of battles fought here, atrocities committed, or anything like the enmity recorded in other parts of the expanding American nation.

Maybe it was the placid nature of orcharding that evolved with its annual cycle of maintenance, harvest, and storage. The abundance of fruit this provided allowed enough for growers to feed themselves, with increasing amounts left over for trade. Or maybe it was the mountains. Shielded by the Cascade foothills that surround it, perhaps the area was blessed by a measure of isolation from tribal warfare and ravaging natural disaster. Then again, it might have been the churches. The earliest non-natives to stay in the area were Catholic missionaries, men who spent decades living out their faith among the Wenatchi. It could be that their peaceful service and coexistence laid the groundwork for the society that followed.

Maybe it was all of those things, or none of them. Regardless, I maintain that Cashmere is unique, for its history records centuries of peaceful fruitfulness, education, and civility—something the rest of this book will illustrate.

Yet the only constant is change, as Heraclitus once said. In the 207 years since Cashmere's first European arrival, the town has, for better or worse, kept abreast of American society in popular culture, technology, and politics. And somehow, it has also retained its identity. Still small. Still intimate. Still agrarian yet cultivated, connected yet apart. It is honest to itself and its roots, with parks christened in honor of Wenatchi chiefs, and canyons named after pioneers.

Admittedly, as has happened to many other American small towns, it may one day become a suburb of nearby burgeoning Wenatchee, or perhaps only a weekend retreat of populous Spokane and Seattle. But for now, it is home most of all to its own: the descendants of the earliest Wenatchi, the sons of foreign immigrants, and the daughters of brave settlers.

One

Nt'wt'c'kum

The first known European to hear the Moses-Columbia language was the Welsh-born David Thompson, an employee of the British fur-trading Northwest Company, who passed through the valley with his band of Catholic Iroquois on July 7, 1811. However, the earliest recorded Europeans to stay in the Cashmere Valley, according to local historian Linda Ingraham, were the French Roman Catholic missionaries Frs. Charles Marie Pandosy, Urban Grassi, and Stephen de Rougé, who arrived around 1856. Thanks to their work, the Catholic Church established two places of worship in the area, an "Indian church" in what is now downtown Cashmere, and a settlers' chapel at the mouth of Mission Creek.

In 1849 (before the arrival of the Catholic missionaries but after the fur-trader Thompson), US Army captain George McClellan, the future commander of the Civil War Army of the Potomac, led a party of scouts through the interior of what was then the Oregon Territory. The operation was under the auspices of McClellan's old Mexican War comrade, future Washington territorial governor Isaac Ingalls Stevens (the man for whom Stevens Pass is named). Among McClellan's party of 61 soldiers, civilians, and 160 pack animals were the geologist, ethnographer, and Harvard lawyer George Gibbs, who recorded much of the surviving history of this expedition, and the East Prussian–born US Army private Gustav Sohon, who is perhaps best known to posterity for numerous stunning lithographs and for penning the first English-Salish dictionary. In the sweltering August of that year, historian Richard Scheurman records, McClellan met with the Yakama chief Kamiakin, an encounter that proves Indian relations did not begin as strained as they would become over the next 160 years. McClellan wrote that Kamiakin "expressed very friendly feelings, and I have no reason to doubt his sincerity for, in a number of instances, he displayed an honesty not often found."

Then, like everywhere in the United States, American culture slowly began to supersede that of the natives in the valley. Just 120 years after the first fur traders passed through Nt'wt'c'kum, the Wenatchi population plummeted from perhaps over a thousand to just six individuals in 1904. Many relocated to the Colville Indian Reservation in north central Washington, others died of European diseases their bodies had no immunity to, and the few who stayed tried to find their new niche in the increasingly settled valley.

Those who remained lived on small plots of land in town or, more commonly, in the canyons that ring the Wenatchee river valley. Some, like the eccentric and jovial Nancy "Old Milly" Nanoquist, made close friendships with the white population. Old Milly lived on the estate of Willis Carey, the co-owner of a local fruit warehouse and the first known European to bear the title *hi-yup*, or "good friend." Others, like Old Milly's contemporary "Old Mollie," lived in a teepee several miles within Ollala Canyon, preferring the solitude the rugged valley allowed. Occasionally, visitors from the Colville Reservation would come to town, but those too dwindled over time. Aside from a few small, annual social gatherings, the Wenatchi became a people all but forgotten in their own home.

That is, until 1931. With the help of local attorney J. Harold Anderson, Mark Balaban of Liberty Orchards, the Cashmere Chamber of Commerce, and many others, the Wenatchi resurged to the forefront of local society with the last great powwow of Nt'wt'c'kum, now in its 27th year as Cashmere. While it had a festival atmosphere to outsiders, the powwow was a more serious affair than most observers realized. Indeed, it is likely the only time that Cashmere has hosted a meeting of international diplomacy. Prominent native elders, such as the centenarian Mary Owhi Moses of Nespelem, along with no less than the governor of Washington, Roland H. Harley, endured the scorching heat of August 20, 21, and 22 to discuss Native-US treaty progress with John Harmelt, last chief of the Wenatchi. Prominent on the agenda was a reenactment of the 76-year-old 1855 Treaty of Yakama, which brought to life multiple federal promises relating to land and fishing rights that had not been honored. Most Wenatchi watching entertained no real hope of this ever changing.

Long after most of those there had passed on, their dreams came to fruition. In 2010, the US Ninth Circuit Court of Appeals, in *United States v. the Confederated Tribes of the Colville Reservation*, ruled that the Wenatchi and Yakama Indians were entitled to unregulated fishing rights in the Wenatchee River at the Wenatshapam Fishery, which is located at the confluence of the Icicle and Wenatchee Rivers in Leavenworth. Seventy-nine years after the powwow concluded, the P'squosa and other native peoples gained the promises of their 155-year-old treaty and returned to the fishing grounds of their ancestors.

Arguably the most precious artifact housed in the Cashmere Valley Museum, this petroglyph may be hundreds—or as much as 13,000—years old. It is a native historical marker, like a diary entry carved in rock, which shows the results of a day's hunt. A horizontal line begins and ends with a circle. The carving is read from left (sunrise) to right (sunset). Two adult figures are clearly visible at right, and a child is possibly depicted near the sunrise symbol. The animals in the carving represent the game that the group took, a full-grown buck.

Chief John Harmelt, who was the last chief of the P'squosa (the Wenatchi), is seen here at the 1931 Cashmere powwow. Chief Harmelt spent much of his adult life litigating with territorial, state, and federal authorities for tribal land and fishing rights, personally negotiating two ratified treaties with the federal government. Sadly, these agreements went unenforced until 2010, seventy-five years after his death in 1935, when his descendants regained their right to unregulated fishing on their traditional lands in Leavenworth, Washington. Harmelt's native name was An Hum-milt. *An* roughly translates to the definite article "the," used in his language as an honorific indicating a position of leadership. This image is from the original negative by Simmer Studios.

In 1900, at approximately 100 years of age, Chief Sil-ah-ko-sasket III sat for this portrait in Entiat, a town north of Cashmere along the Columbia River. A prominent leader of the Entiat, a subordinate band of the Wenatchi, Sil-ah-ko-sasket was one of the wealthiest native leaders in the greater Wenatchee Valley. The Wenatchi concept of wealth was most often measured in heads of horse, of which no local was Sil-ah-ko-sasket's equal. In addition to perhaps several hundred horses, he reportedly had at least three wives and as many as 50 children. He made a practice of enriching himself by offering his daughters as wives to local settlers in exchange for a dowry of steeds. This image is from an original negative, perhaps taken by Simmer Studios.

GEN'L. GEO. B. McCLELLAN.

Entered according to Act of Congress in the year 1861, by M. B. Brady, in the Clerks' office of the District Court of the District of Columbia.

Maj. Gen. George B. McClellan, known to history as the commanding general of the Army of the Potomac during the Civil War from 1861 to 1863, was even better known as the arrogant officer President Lincoln fired for his repeated strategic failures. However, nine years prior to the war, as a captain in the summer of 1853, McClellan was the first to make official contact with the Wenatchi, camping with them on the sandy flats at what is now the eastern end of the Odabashian Bridge in East Wenatchee. According to the historian Richard Scheuerman in *The Wenatchee Valley: And its First Peoples*, Captain McClellan was a skillful and genteel negotiator who exchanged gifts and forged an unusually candid and friendly relationship with tribal leaders. Unfortunately, later representatives of the United States acted with markedly less decency, plunging American, Washington, and Wenatchi relationships into more than a century of distrust and hostility. (Courtesy of the Abraham Lincoln Gettysburg Blog.)

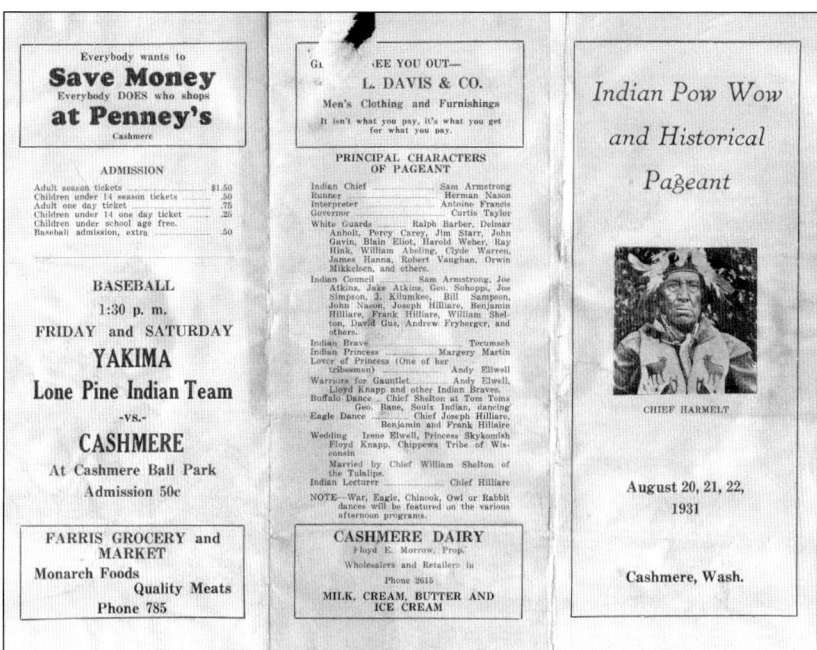

This is the program for the last grand powwow of the Wenatchi Indians, held in Cashmere August 20–22, 1931. The City of Cashmere and tribal leaders organized the powwow near the entrance to Mission Creek on the southern end of town as a tribute to the Wenatchi people. John Harmelt, last chief of the Wenatchi, was the guest of honor. The powwow was a tremendous event, with nearly every resident of Cashmere, Indian and otherwise, attending. It featured horseracing, ceremonial dancing, music, and traditional games of chance using Wenatchi "gambling bones." The gambling bone game was an extended affair, often taking all day. It involved repeated betting sessions decided by the casting of dice-like, etched animal bones.

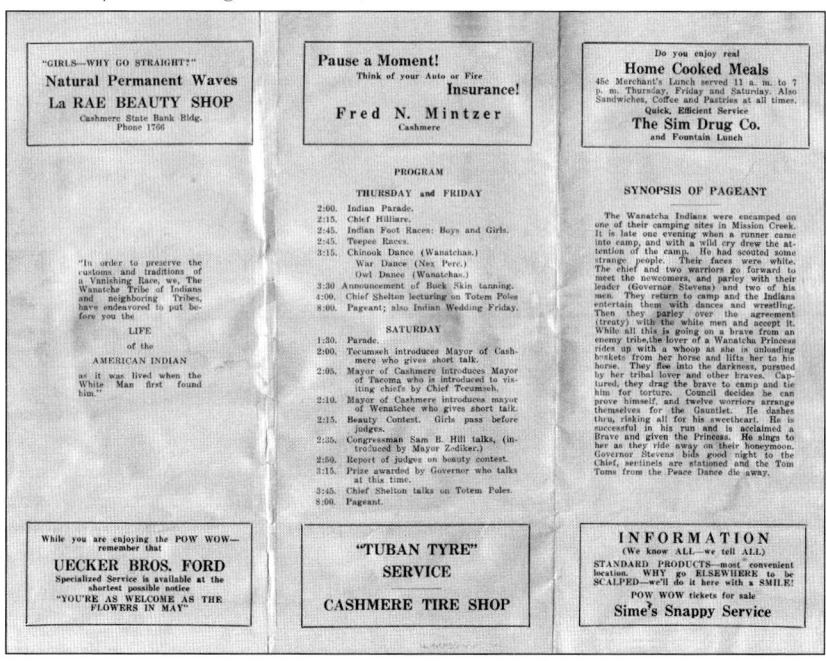

Chief John Harmelt is shown here at the height of his influence. Guest of honor at the 1931 Cashmere powwow and last chief of the Wenatchi, the 89-year-old was the son of William (How-milt) and Monique of Pine Flat (what is today Dryden). His first wife, who died early, was Celia Ann (Towhamsees), known to non-Indians as "Annie." His second wife was a widow, or possibly a divorcée, named Ellen (Qui-hon-meeh't), the daughter of Old Yaxsum (Tyeahkin) and Anastasia (Klikitcha) of Yaksum Canyon in Cashmere. Harmelt died in 1935, four years after this photograph was taken. (Courtesy of the Wenatchee Valley Museum and Cultural Center.)

The 1931 Cashmere powwow was equal parts diplomatic summit, fair, and religious holiday. This photograph shows Indians performing a ritual dance, a spectacle that blurred the lines between the mundane and the sacred. Festivities and trade were intermixed with serious treaty-related discussions under the auspices of Chief Harmelt, while other leaders took charge of social and cultural events. (Courtesy of the Wenatchee Valley Museum and Cultural Center.)

Antonine Francis, also known as Antonine Adkins (or "Atkins"), is here mistakenly labeled "Antoine." Antonine, who belonged to the Entiat band of the Wenatchi, like Sil-ah-ko-sasket III, is shown here in his regalia at Cashmere's last powwow. At powwows, bands of the Wenatchi and outside tribes would bring goods to trade, eligible youngsters for betrothal, and fiancés ready for their marriage ceremonies. Antonine, who was married several times, probably said at least one of his nuptial vows at a ceremony much like this one. This image is from the original negative by Simmer Studios.

From left to right in this c. 1910 photograph are Cistine Antonine (likely related to Antonine Francis), Casteen Felix (related to Mary Felix [Pux-eel], shown in later pictures), and Yach-pu-mox, the mother of Josephic Estes. Like many of the Wenatchi, beyond the most famous, little is known about these women other than their names. (Courtesy of the Wenatchee Valley Museum and Cultural Center.)

Antonine Francis, right, is pictured here with his wife Mary Lou (Pakotas) at the 1931 Cashmere powwow. The totem pole, like the feathered regalia and the teepees, is not native to the Columbia Plateau Indians, including the Wenatchi. The ceremonial attire and tentage shown in many of these powwow pictures were cultural borrowings from the Plains Indians, and the totem pole is an artifact from the coastal Indians of the Pacific Northwest. This particular pole was a gift from the Snohomish chief Shelton, who personally carved it. Shelton was a highly honored guest at the powwow, traveling from the Tulalip Reservation in western Washington.

This is the home of Antonine Francis in Mission, who is shown with his first known wife, Ellen. The photograph dates from around 1902, twenty-nine years before the Cashmere powwow. Francis had an orchard and a blacksmith shop, both of which can be seen here. From left to right are Francis; Mary Felix (Pux-eel), holding the infant Joe Adkins (an alternate surname of Francis's); Josephine (T'wha-whee-ah-so), Francis's mother; the infant Jake Adkins (sitting on the ground); and Ellen (Qui-hon-meeh't), Francis's wife (and later the second wife of Chief Harmelt) by the door. As the many names for the same individuals clearly show, early 20th century Wenatchi did not take great care with their English monikers. They viewed them as impersonal, inferior identities only adopted to better deal with the settler population. As such, multiple names for the same person, multiple spellings of the same name, and identical names across generations are very common. (Courtesy of Joe Atkins and the Wenatchee Valley Museum and Cultural Center.)

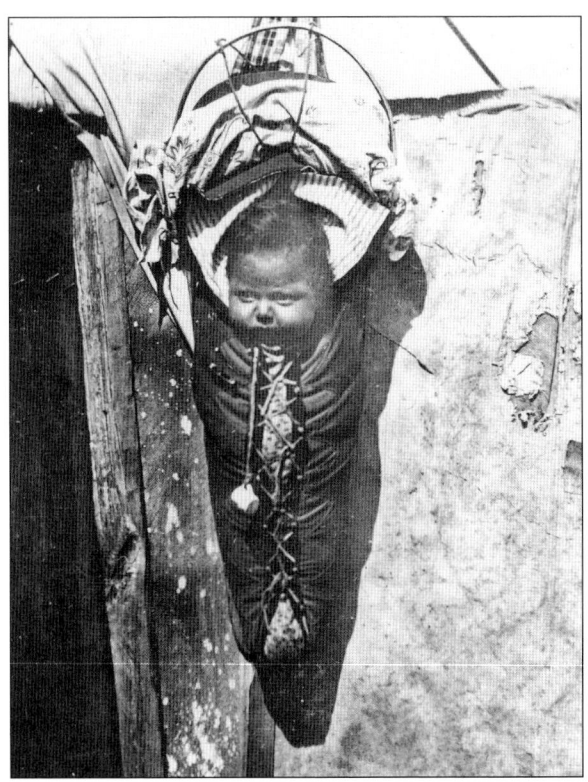

Pictured here at the 1931 Cashmere powwow is the about 18-month-old Annie (Pakotas), who was perhaps named in honor of the previously mentioned Mary Lou (Pakotas). This young girl is snug in the cradleboard that her mother, Ellen Adkins (Qui-hon-meeh't), made with her own hands. (Courtesy of the Bernice Gellatly Greene Photography Collection and the Wenatchee Valley Museum and Cultural Center.)

At right is Ellen Adkins, mother of the previously pictured baby Annie (Pakotas). One of Adkins's tribal names, in addition to Qui-hon-meeh't, was Such-tatq, and in her arms is her infant Vincent, the son of Harry (Pe-el), seated at left. It is unclear why Annie is not in the photograph. Behind Ellen and Vincent is Harry's aunt Annie Kitsap. Harry was Ellen's third husband, directly following Allen Adkins, a white man who was Ellen's husband after her divorce from Antonine Francis. This is another example of the confusion stemming from the Indians' use of English names as mere "go-bys" only meant for their occasional dealings with outsiders, combined with multiple marriages. (Courtesy of the Wenatchee Valley Museum and Cultural Center.)

Prominent elder Mary Felix poses in authentic Wenatchi regalia in a staged hide-tanning scene along Mission Creek in Cashmere. The traditional Wenatchi tanning method was to treat the hide of an animal in its own brains, which would be boiled down and mashed into a paste before being applied. At that time, one animal's brains were enough to tan its entire hide, but modern ranching practices have altered the ratio of cowhide to brain matter to the point that it would take the heads of several animals to replicate this ancient method. This image is from the original negative by Simmer Studios.

"Chief" Kiutus Tecumseh (pronounced tee-CUHM-see) and Mary Felix display a parfleche. Parfleches were a type of shield, the name of which derives from the French *parer*, "to ward off," and *fleche*, "arrow." French trappers were among the first Europeans in the Nt'wt'c'kum area, arriving in the early to mid-1800s, and introduced the term. Contrary to local popular belief, Tecumseh was not really a chief, and Cashmere Museum curator Fred Harvey questions if he was even a Wenatchi; regardless, in later life, Tecumseh portrayed himself as a tribal leader and used that fraudulent image to secure a position as spokesman for Skookum Apples. The woven hat Mary Felix wears in this picture was traditional Wenatchi headwear, starkly juxtaposed with the ostentatious Plains Indian headdresses Kiutus Tecumseh often wore to help sell his persona. This image is from the original negative by Simmer Studios.

From left to right in this 1931 photograph are Frank Galler, Pete Judge, and Kiutus Tecumseh. Note the swastika on the teepee. The origins of this symbol are at least 5,000 years more ancient than its use by Adolf Hitler's Nazi Party from 1920 to 1945, and may have their ultimate beginnings in the Indian subcontinent. The word *swastika* is derived from the Sanskrit *svastika*, which roughly translates as "good fortune" or "well-being." The symbol is thought to have been created in the New Stone Age, and its prevalence in Salish and other native cultures lends credence to the Asian origin theory of Native Americans. This image is from the original negative by Simmer Studios.

The westward expansion of settlers drove many formerly disparate tribes of Native Americans into greater contact. One result of this, like feathered headdresses, was the loan of the teepee from Plains Indian culture to the Columbia Plateau peoples. These teepees were set up for the 1931 powwow. (Courtesy of the Wenatchee Valley Museum and Cultural Center.)

In this image, also taken at the 1931 powwow, the two women on the right are wearing the distinctive headgear of the Columbia Plateau tribes, to which the Wenatchi belong. While the masculine feathered headdresses, the most famous of regalia, were cultural borrowings, the women's woven, fez-like hats were unique to central Washington. (Courtesy of the Wenatchee Valley Museum and Cultural Center.)

The same woman who is pictured at right in the previous photograph is featured here in one of the many stunning images captured by the early 20th-century photographer Alfred G. Simmer. By the summer of 1931, when this was taken, Simmer had shot 5,783 developed pictures, many of which have become testimonies of the unique history of the Cashmere Valley. (Courtesy of the Wenatchee Valley Museum and Cultural Center.)

This 1931 powwow photograph shows the last Wenatchi shaman, Johnny Baker, in regalia along with a woven basket. Baker would have been responsible for his people's physical and spiritual well-being, though by this time most took advantage of western medicine. As with pottery in ancient Eurasia, baskets like the one shown here were both functional and artistic to the Wenatchi. Specific motifs were passed along familial lines, and individual households could be differentiated by their basketry alone. (Courtesy of the Wenatchee Valley Museum and Cultural Center.)

Mary Baker was the daughter of Johnny Baker. As time wore on, western modernity came to the Cashmere Indian community. Baker's tribal name was Ah-leel-tum, but she was better known to the European community as "Big Mary." Her daughter Maryann (Tee-emptq), standing behind her brother on the left, went by "Little Mary." Baker's two young boys, from left to right, were Edward Alexander (Tope) and Michael (Palk-ay-ocksha).

Shown here is the Yakama family matriarch Mary Ohwi Moses, daughter of Yakama chief Ohwi and widow of Columbia Indians chief Moses (from whom the name of the Wenatchi language, Moses-Columbia, is derived). Mary Moses attended the 1931 powwow in her relative Louie Friedlander's 1924 Nash automobile, a vehicle that, according to Richard Scheurman in *The Wenatchee Valley: And its First Peoples*, she derisively called an "iron horse on wheels." Mary's father, husband, and brother, the warrior Qualchan, all died near Wenatchee in combat with a detachment of US Army soldiers under the command of Maj. Robert S. Garnett. (Courtesy of the Wenatchee Valley Museum and Cultural Center.)

Mary Moses, approximately 100 years old at the time of the 1931 Cashmere powwow, sits in front of her granddaughter Nellie Hilburn (Nellie Kamiakin Friedlander), with, on the left, Lucy Friedlander (later, Lucy Covington) and, at right, Lucy's sister Emily Peone. Though men most often held the positions of highest leadership in Columbia Plateau Indian society, women were far from shrinking violets. Mary Moses exercised great leadership and influenced many others within the Colville Reservation. (Courtesy of the Wenatchee Valley Museum and Cultural Center.)

The two young women shown here went on to be powerful in the leadership of the Colville Confederated Tribes, the political entity that governs the Colville Indian Reservation. On the left is 21-year-old Lucy Friedlander, who gained particular prominence advocating for natives with the federal government, and on the right is her sister, the future Colvillle elder Emily Peone. They are the great-granddaughters of Wenatchi matriarch Mary Owhi Moses, widow of Chief Moses. In preparation for the 1931 powwow, Emily was questioned whether they should allow their grandmother to go to Cashmere. Richard Scheurman, in *The Wenatchee Valley: And its First Peoples*, records her as responding, "How could we not take her? She may have been over a hundred, but she still ruled the family. We were the ones who needed her permission!" (Courtesy of the Wenatchee Valley Museum and Cultural Center.)

Emily Peone, sister of Lucy Friedlander and a future tribal elder, rides through Yaksum Canyon at the 1931 powwow. The horse was introduced to the Wenatchi sometime around the year 1730 through contact with the Plains Indians of southern Idaho. Though archaeological records show that horses lived in North America in prehistory, they were extinct long before the arrival of native peoples from Asia and were reintroduced with Spanish incursions into Mexico. (Courtesy of the Wenatchee Valley Museum and Cultural Center.)

From right to left, Lucy (Friedlander) Covington is shown with tribal members Mel Tonasket and Shirley Palmer. Lucy was of mixed Wenatchi and German-Jewish heritage and went on to be a national leader in Indian advocacy. As reported by Jim Camden of the *Spokane Spokesman-Review*, she was honored in 2015 as the namesake of a center for Native American students at Eastern Washington University. (Courtesy of Mel Tonasket and the Wenatchee Valley Museum and Cultural Center.)

Dying in 1932 at 102 years of age, "Old Mollie" (native name Mishe-e Twa, alternatively Misheetwie and "Indian Mollie") was a skilled Wenatchi beader who traded with the local settler population. This c. 1929 photograph was taken at the mouth of the Nahahum Canyon in Cashmere. In the background is her house, a wood and tule mat lodge covered with animal skins. The tule is a type of bulrush, also known as a cattail, prevalent along central Washington's rivers, and is a traditional Wenatchi building material. This image is from the original negative by Willis Carey.

Old Mollie, mounted, rides alongside her friend Doris. Mollie lived on an allotment, which in this case meant a parcel of land allocated to one person but owned by another. Her home was a teepee approximately two and a half miles into Olalla Canyon in Cashmere. She was the sister of Clotilda Judge (Ti-sa-qt) and Kami Sam and is buried in the Cashmere Indian Cemetery just north of the current site of Apple Annie's Antique Gallery. This cemetery is now largely overlooked and in poor repair, with several decades passing since the last Indian was laid to rest there. (Courtesy of the Wenatchee Valley Museum and Cultural Center.)

On the left in this c. 1915 photograph is Clotilda Judge (Ti-sa-qt) beside her sister Old Mollie, both of the Wenatchi. Clotilda was the sister of Kami Sam, who lived in Mission Creek, and the mother of Louie Judge, who lived in Jude Canyon, near Leavenworth. Mollie, a spinster, was well known in the local community, especially through her friendship with local fruit magnate Willis Carey. (Courtesy of the Wenatchee Valley Museum and Cultural Center)

Nancy Nanoquist was locally known as "Old Milly." Often confused with her contemporary "Old Mollie," Old Milly was a weaver and beader well-known in Cashmere for her gregarious manners, frequently joking raucously with Mission townspeople. She had a close but platonic relationship with orchardist Willis Carey (1880–1955) and built her lodge on his land. This image is from the original negative by Willis Carey.

Pete Judge, the son of Louis and Baptistine Judge, is approximately 16 in this 1932 photograph. He was among the first Wenatchi to complete his primary education in the Cashmere School District and attend university. Note again the non-native feathered headdress. While quite a few took on these Plains Indian fashions willingly, Cashmere Museum curator Fred Harvey attests that many Wenatchi sat for photographs in this affected garb solely to meet outsiders' expectations of how an Indian should look. This image is from the original negative by Willis Carey.

US Army private Ayapith P. Judge, like many local Native Americans, was a friend of Willis Carey's. Beloved among the local Indians, Carey gained the affectionate title of *hi-yup*, or "good friend." This signed photograph from Judge is dated November 27, 1942, when America's involvement in World War II was less than a year old. The inscription reads, "To Mr and Mrs Willis Carey, best wishes, Ayapith P. Judge, November 27, 1942. U.S. Army." Judge sending it to Carey is a testament that their relationship was important enough to write home in the midst of a war, likely just before reporting to his permanent duty station.

Kiutus Tecumseh's potato field is pictured in a World War II–era *Cashmere Valley Record* article. Tecumseh's field was a "defense garden," a wartime subsistence farm designed to ease a family's need for commercially bought food (though Tecumseh intended to sell his produce to the US Army). Tecumseh, despite his untruthful claims of being a Wenatchi chief, was an honorably disabled World War I veteran. Sometime after the 1931 powwow, he converted the celebration's grounds into his personal field. He was always a showman, and a *Cashmere Valley Record* article noted that "the Chief is posing in the picture to show how he has laid aside his war clothes to work for victory." Tecumseh went on to attribute his garden's yield, which was apparently substantial, to "continually singing to the potatoes and carrots."

At far right is Cashmere's patron of local history, Willis Carey. The vast majority of the Native American artifacts housed in the Cashmere Museum today were his donations, which he generally received as gifts from the friends he made in the local Wenatchi community. Fond of entertaining and celebrating local culture, and being a fruit-warehousing mogul with the means to afford it, Willis is shown here in regalia inside of his "Hobby House." He donated his collection to the city on the condition it be properly displayed, an arrangement that ultimately led to the creation of the Cashmere Museum.

Two

MISSION

In 1889, the first post office opened in Mission, the settler name that had come to replace Nt'wt'c'kum, and the establishment of this building meant that the town's new name was official. The name was now entered into the administrative registries of America and the newly formed state of Washington. The name was most likely derived from Mission Creek, the body of water flowing north from the Wenatchee Mountains near the site of one of the two first Catholic churches in town.

By 1889, first settler Alexander Brender had been in town 20 years and was the namesake of a canyon and creek on the west end of town. He built a house several miles up Brender Canyon and began to farm, later replacing subsistence crops with fruit trees after D.S. Farrar, credited with being the valley's first orchardist, arrived in 1883. Brender and his wife, Samantha, raised Bramlett, Lassie, and Georgia Trout, Samantha's Texas-born children by her first marriage, as well as their own locally born children Charles, Henry, Jesse, and Peter, in the shadow of what is today called Stine's Hill, Needlepoint, or more recently, Tower Mountain.

As these children grew, Alexander and Samantha welcomed new settlers to their town. These families flowed into the area seeking the 160 free acres promised to settlers under the 1862 Homestead Act. Newcomers like William Bourgwardt, Matt Green, Denis Strong, O.C. McManus, and Reuben A. Brown found good timber and fertile, albeit dry, ground with a predictable climate that allowed for consistent fruit growing.

Still, the living was harsh. According to Laura Arksey of HistoryLink, manufactured goods only came over from Ellensburg via Blewett Pass, which was fraught with danger even into the automobile era, or through the port of Wenatchee along the Columbia River. No bridges crossed the Wenatchee River, the largest body of water in Mission. It was too swift and shallow for ferries and only fordable at certain areas. Still, the valley's spare hills eventually gave way to cultivated fields, leveled plots, and even a general store. The canyons turned green with irrigation, and honeybees dominated the air when the newly planted apple trees burst into bloom.

In 1892, the full thrust of American civilization came to Mission with the arrival of the Great Northern Railway, an event that residents John F. Woodring and I.W. Sherman used as the impetus to legally plat the town. Though much development had occurred since Father Grassi's first encounter with the P'squosa 36 years earlier, this was unquestionably the point when Mission turned from uncharted wilderness into the settled West. It was no longer isolated by foreboding forests or raging rivers, but connected directly to the increasingly urban Puget Sound and the powerful industries of the American East.

Not surprisingly, this transition fueled dramatic change. Mission's postal service, increasingly reliant on the railway, had operated only with difficulty since 1889. John Woodring, the first postmaster, frequently received complaints from locals furious that their inbound letters routinely ended up in those *other* towns named Mission, particularly one settlement over a hundred miles to the southeast. Woodring therefore likely welcomed local judge James H. Chase's suggestion to rename the town Cashmere, a nod to Thomas Moore's 1817 novel *Lalla Rookh*. Chase compared Mission's beauty to Moore's depiction of the Vale of Kashmir in India, and the townspeople agreed. Mission became Cashmere on July 1, 1904, and its homage to the Himalayan region continues today in the names of its institutions, most notably the Cashmere School District's Vale Elementary.

Alexander Bartolomäus Brender was the first non-missionary to settle in Mission. Brender was born on August 24, 1851, in Giengen an der Brenz in the Kingdom of Württemberg (modern-day southwest Germany). Fleeing a Europe still smarting from the Napoleonic wars and the German wars of unification, Brender followed other German immigrants to the Washington Territory and encouraged his uncle Johann Brender, then in Eudora, Kansas, to join him in the greater Wenatchee Valley. (Courtesy of the *Cashmere Valley Record*.)

The sons of Alexander Bartolomäus Brender, from left to right, were Henry Bart, Jesse, Charlie, and Pete. They grew up with their siblings Bramlett, Lassie, and Georgia Trout, the children by a former spouse of Alexander's wife, Samantha (Warren) Trout. Trout was a widow from Erath County, Texas, whom the owner of an Ellensburg trading post had told Brender about. Brender had been eight years a bachelor in America by that point, and he made arrangements to bring Samantha and her family to central Washington after nothing but correspondence. The day she arrived in Ellensburg was the first time that they met in person—and the day they were married. Brender's descendants lived on Alexander's original homestead property, albeit not in the original house, until the early 2000s, when Melvin "Bud" Brender and his wife, Esther, sold the land to neighbor Jim Willems, who in turn sold it to Seattle restaurateurs Ludger and Julie Szamania. The Szamanias converted the house to a bed-and-breakfast and its orchard into a vineyard. Capitalizing on this history, the Brender family rented the building and held the majority of their 2010 reunion on the property.

Dating to sometime between 1893 and 1898, this photograph is the oldest known picture of Mission. Taken by Welden Burgess, it shows the Presbyterian church (third building from right), constructed in 1893, but not the Mission Hotel, which was built in 1898. The town's earliest structures were almost universally built along the railroad line, and the cluster near center is opposite the site of the present-day railroad depot, near the Aplets & Cotlets retail store. In 1892, the proportion of Wenatchi Indians to settlers was a commanding 350 to 6, though this would be irrevocably reversed in the coming decades.

Most likely taken in the late 1890s, this photograph shows Abbie Cobb (left) and Eula Fisher, residents of Mission Creek, posing in dresses designed by Jessie (Rodkey) Bell, wife of A.C. Jones, the first mayor of Mission.

Shown here is a view looking west from the top of Flowery Divide, also called "Needlepoint," toward Dryden, Peshastin, and Leavenworth. Flowery Divide is a large ridgeline on the western edge of town that geologists theorize was at least partially created during the Missoula Flood near the end of the last ice age. This flood is thought to have covered the Cashmere Valley in as much as 800 feet of water.

This is the Cashmere Museum's replica of the Roman Catholic Francis Xavier Mission, named after St. Francis Xavier, cofounder of the Jesuit order. The actual church was one of the first—and possibly the first—structures built in Cashmere. It was located near the mouths of Yaksum Canyon and Mission Creek. The actual mission burned down three times, but the replica has so far escaped its predecessors' fates.

In this 1896 photograph of the railroad line near Mission, the large boulder, which had fallen onto the track, is a chunk of sandstone estimated to weigh 125 tons. Railroad workers used 110 pounds of dynamite to remove it.

Shown here is the Mission Post Office around 1900. From left to right are an unidentified man (on the far side of the counter), Anna Manson, Dick Manson, and Archie Manson. At the time of its founding, Mission was part of Kittitas County, and the original postal building was located in Walter Olive's hardware store. It later occupied a two-story building on Mission Street, where it was also used as an office for the Columbia Valley Lumber Company, the Columbia Lumber Company, and the Potlatch Lumber Company. The Mission postal service, under Postmaster John F. Woodring, was a key factor in the town's name being changed to Cashmere. This change was necessitated by the tremendous amount of misdirected mail caused by so many towns in the young state of Washington being named Mission. The post office moved to the Grange Building in 1912.

The Cashmere Post Office is pictured here around 1920. This facility was on the ground floor of the original Grange Building, at the intersection of Cottage Avenue and Woodring Street. In the service window are Archie Manson, right, and an unidentified woman.

Though not technically Cashmere, Monitor, the town's next-door-neighbor to the east, deserves mention for the fame of L.J. "Jack" Richardson's land, pictured here when his family first claimed it as a homestead. Immediately turned into an orchard, this ground was where the Richared variety of the Red Delicious apple first mutated from its parent stock. Richardson won the 1951 American Pomological Society's Wilder Medal for the cultivar's outstanding merit. He responded, "It's a big honor. It's the Nobel Peace Prize of fruit." The Richared later also spawned the Royalred variety in the orchard of Walter Plough of Wenatchee in 1952.

The Jarchow & Johnson department store was located at 120 Cottage Avenue. It was one of the town's earliest downtown structures and was first recorded in the *Cashmere Valley Record* in 1902. This building burned in 1928 when, according to local legend, a passing train threw a spark onto nearby wooden construction. The present-day Henry Building was built in its place in 1929.

Shown here is Cottage Avenue, in a view looking west in 1910. The first building on the right is the Cascade Garage, the site of present-day Clifford's Hardware. The Cascade Garage was the first Ford dealership in the still-new Chelan County, which was formed out of Kittitas County in 1899. The garage was owned by W.B. and F.W. Paton, who demolished the structure and built a new one at the same location in 1913. Opposite the garage, the first building on the left is the Jarchow & Johnson general store. Third on the left is the Pastime Stationery & Confectionary, and in the background stand the two banks that were then in town.

Roy Kooken (left) and Bert Hanson stand on Division Street in 1918. The two-story building behind them was built in 1907 as the Cottage Opera House; after later serving as the Estes-Hanan Realty Company, it was converted to a café, a hotel, and then a rest home.

Pete Hanson, born in 1875, is pictured here with his general store, the Pastime Stationery and Confectionary, at 116 Cottage Avenue. F.C. Ardon, F.A. Ardon, and Frank E. Schmitten founded the store in 1909. Pete was the oldest son of Erick A. Hanson, a former steamboat captain on the Columbia River. His business later became the Pastime Tavern and finally the Rendezvous.

THE OLD SWIMMING HOLE · CASHMERE · WASH · ADAHEN · 138-V.

"Big Rock" and the "old swimming hole" used to be just slightly upstream from the present-day Cashmere Museum. The downstream waters near the stone were calm and provided a relatively safe place for children and adults to swim. Upstream from the rock about 100 yards was a small island in the Wenatchee River popular for camping. The Washington State Department of Transportation used the island as landfill in 1958 when the construction of Highway 2 required earth to reinforce the Wenatchee's banks.

Ed Hinman, an early schoolteacher in Mission, sat for this portrait in 1897. Hinman, H.G. "Dandy" Bills, and O.C. McManus hewed and moved the logs for the school where Hinman taught. The school's original location was near the mouth of Brender Canyon in 1889; it is unsurprising that Hinman Drive, near Brender Canyon on the west end of town, was named in his honor.

The Brender Schoolhouse, where Ed Hinman taught, is shown at its original location at the mouth of Brender Canyon. After many years of service, the one-room structure was repurposed as a woodsman's meeting hall, and later as a private residence. Around 1969, the building was disassembled and moved to the Cashmere Museum grounds. Unfortunately, the reconstruction was inadvertently flawed when builders put only one window on the left side of the school where originally there were two. In the background are the men's and women's outhouses.

In 2010, the modern-day relatives of Alexander Brender gathered in Cashmere for a family reunion (sleeping nights in the bed-and-breakfast that was once his homestead). While they were touring the Cashmere Museum during their first full day, curator Fred Harvey, a key resource for this book, invited them to sit in the very Brender Schoolhouse that many of their ancestors had sat in 120 years before. From left to right are US Army colonel Arnold Brender, medical doctor; Douglas Brender, Woodinville area schoolteacher and son of Bob Brender, former mayor of Leavenworth; Linda (Fullenwider) Brender, his wife; Ulrike (Brender) Nothnick, retired Christian youth leader from Germany; US Army captain L. Burton Brender, author of this book and co-host of the 2010 reunion (along with his wife, Elizabeth [St. George]); Bernd Nothnick, husband to Ulrike and also a retired Christian youth leader from Germany; Marilyn (Brender) Kuczborski, from Michigan; Gerald Toler; and Lynn (Brender) Toler, his wife.

The Cashmere Volunteer Fire Department is seen in front of the "Old G.A.R. [Grand Army of the Republic] Building" around 1900. This space was later occupied by the Farmers & Merchants Bank and is now the site of the Cashmere Valley Bank. Being one of the larger structures in town, it originally doubled as a meeting hall and, interestingly, was not torn down when the Farmers & Merchants was built in 1909 but simply moved to the west end of its lot. The building later became the Hupmobile auto dealership from 1911 to 1912 and was last mentioned in the *Cashmere Valley Record* as the Electric Machine Shop in 1913.

In a view looking north from Division Street, the Cashmere Volunteer Fire Department conducts training in front of the Big Department Store, built in 1906, and the Ellis Ford Co. department store, also known as "the Big Store." Brothers W.H. and E.C. Mills were the original board members of "the Big D." Over the years, they took on other businesses and in 1911 bought out the Ellis Ford store, thereby owning their former competition. The Big Store became Mills Bros. Dept. Store and then the Cashmere Mercantile after W.H. Mills retired. It is unclear whether this Mills Bros. was related to the long-lived fine clothing store in Wenatchee of the same name, which was opened under brothers Sam and Harvey Mills in 1906 and ran for 110 years. In 1915, the Big Store burned and today the eastern half of its ruined structure is part of the Pratt Chiropractic clinic. These two stores were the precursors of the shopping district now located at the intersection of Division Street and Cottage Avenue.

The Mission Hotel was built along Mission Street in 1898 and demolished in 1927 to make way for Cashmere City Hall. In 1905, the Mission Hotel faced competition from the Cashmere Hotel, which directly marketed to railway travelers and was later renamed the Blewett Hotel. Today, the site is the city hall parking lot.

S.P. Beecher rides a single horse-drawn buggy around 1900. Credited as the owner of Springdale Orchards in nearby Peshastin, he would have carted his fruit to the train depot in Mission, or possibly Leavenworth, on its way to urban markets in Seattle, Spokane, or farther east.

This photograph of Mission's first road grading crew was mailed from Matt to George and Gertie around the turn of the 20th century. On the back, Matt identifies himself as the man with his hand in front of his face at far left. He describes the machine as a 10-horse grader, staged in front of "the church." This piece of equipment had recently been used to repair a canyon road; from

Matt's writing, it was the second photograph taken of the crew. These pictures were possibly intended to serve as a painter's model as, according to Matt, "the artist wanted a picture of our ten horse and the old grader."

Mission in the early 20th century witnessed firsthand the overlap between the ancient technology of the horse and the modern automobile. For a time, the town's wide dirt streets bore both. One of the two men in this photograph is Claude Clark, though which is lost to time.

Pictured here are drays, or freight wagons, which hauled goods from Mission's rail station into town, or perhaps ventured as far west as the bustling train depot of Leavenworth or east to the river port of Wenatchee. While locomotives and steamboats moved goods to and from the country's urban centers, drays such as these were used to complete the final stretch of the journey from retailer to home.

Though not taken in Mission, this photograph of the *Selkirk*, a Columbia River steamboat based out of nearby Wenatchee, is relevant because of the economic and travel link it provided to local residents. The produce of Mission found markets in remote settlements up and down the Columbia River thanks to steamboats such as this, which provided relatively safe and easy movement through the rugged interior of Washington State.

This photograph shows the Woods family, about which unfortunately little is known. At left is Mrs. Woods, and the two at right are unidentified. Though the image is undated, the clothing places it near the turn of the 20th century.

Pictured here are Dan Woods and his wife. If this photograph dates from around the year 1900, the photographer could well have used a Kodak Brownie, a large, box-shaped camera that was inexpensive enough to be widely available. Camera technology at the turn of the 20th century had advanced to the point where subjects no longer had to sit still for protracted periods, allowing for the slightly more natural expression seen on Mrs. Woods's face.

Mrs. Woods is pictured here standing in the center of the back row. The other women are not identified, and could have been family members or friends made through the town's civic organizations, such as the Rotary or, if this image dates from after 1906, the women's Minerva Club. The Minerva Club debated literature, planned community involvement, and provided a place for women to socialize outside of family and church.

Dan Woods, standing next to the horse, and his family were ostensibly orchardists. Notice the thick, bushy nature of the fruit tree in the background, a relic of earlier growing methods that did not heavily prune or shape trees to be less tall.

This is a winter scene of mid-Brender Canyon, looking northwest from what is now Sky Meadows Road. The views that the western hilltops in Cashmere provide of the Cascade Mountains in the west and the upper Wenatchee Valley to the east are absolutely breathtaking. (Courtesy of the *Cashmere Valley Record*.)

This is the first Schmitten Lumber Company site in Brender Canyon in 1902, the year of its opening. Lumber was a key industry in Mission both for use locally and for sale to distant urban centers. The facility no longer exists, but the venerable Schmitten family does. Founder F.W. Schmitten's descendant Ray Schmitten, a Cashmere orchardist, provided the foreword for this book. (Courtesy of Rollie Schmitten and the *Cashmere Valley Record*.)

Cashmere mayor and former judge James H. Chase and his wife are standing in the Highline Railroad Tunnel in the Cascade Range's Snoqualmie Pass in the early 1900s. James Chase is locally famous as the man who changed the name of Mission to Cashmere in homage to Thomas Moore's book *Lalla Rookh*. The tale of East Indian romance references the beautiful Vale of Kashmir. Chase Street in Cashmere is named after Mayor Chase.

Three

CASHMERE

Mission became Cashmere on July 1, 1904, and the name change signaled a new phase in the town's modernity. According to Laura Arksey of HistoryLink, that same year the community welcomed Harry J. Martin, its first medical doctor, and planted its first elms and poplars along its streets (a trend that in 1986 culminated with Cashmere being inducted into the Arbor Day Foundation's Tree City USA program). In 1906, Cashmere residents founded the Minerva Club, a women's society, and over the next 48 months the Rotary, Grange, American Legion, and Boy Scouts joined the town's civic stage. In 1907, the venerable *Cashmere Valley Record* published the first issue of its unbroken, 112-year run, and then, in 1910, the town came on line with its first telephone. From 1910 to 1919, Cashmere electrified its lights, paved its roadways, and celebrated its school system's 20th year of operation.

The town's orchard economy boomed under the consistent irrigation delivered by the 1901 Peshastin Ditch. According to the *The Coast* magazine (October 1906), a single year's harvest produced 135 railcar loads of fruit, an abundance that fueled several supporting businesses. Railway management, hospitality, and lumber production all thrived by virtue of the wealth that the fruit industry brought in. In 1902, Frederick Schmitten opened the first of his sawmills in Brender Canyon, followed by his second in 1910, both of which created major sources of local employment. Cashmere's agricultural production continued to climb as orchardists became more numerous and adept, reinforcing the region's later boast of being the "Apple Capital of the World." Today, the region's fruit reach is truly worldwide, and this author has personally seen local produce on sale as far away as Dongducheon, South Korea, in 2012 and Riyadh, Saudi Arabia, in 2015.

As the town grew increasingly connected, though, it also became embroiled in the apocalyptic conflicts that ravaged the first half of the 20th century. During World Wars I and II, Cashmere stoically shared in the nation's glories and sorrow in Europe, Africa, and Asia. Men and women enlisted or received their draft notices to serve in the ranks of the American armed forces, which mobilized out of Camp Lewis in Tacoma, west of the mountains. And though relatively few people from Cashmere deployed in either conflict, compared to more populous areas, nearly everyone who stayed behind contributed to America's wartime production.

As reported in the *Cashmere Valley Record*, the candy company Aplets & Cotlets canned food for the War Department during World War I, and doughboy veteran Kiutus Tecumseh, the hired spokesman for Skookum Apples, later grew potatoes for the US Army in his defense garden during World War II. Cashmere even manned an aerial lookout tower on Olive Street for the entire duration of World War II, though no enemy flyer ever ventured anywhere close to central Washington.

In 1953, while America was involved in the Korean War, Cashmere celebrated a small home-front victory when it won the privilege of permanently hosting the Chelan County Fair. Though modest in its original construction, and almost scuttled by a tragic jockey death in 1970, the fairgrounds along Kimber Road became a major social gathering point for the entire region. In addition to annual county festivities, the facilities went on to host indoor sports competitions, festivals, outdoor concerts, and private gatherings year-round. Perhaps most importantly, though, the youth of Cashmere have a special love for the fairgrounds, which have been the site of many a first carnival ride, rodeo, and love.

From its earliest days, Cashmere has placed special emphasis on the education of its youth. Having provided organized schooling for more than 130 continuous years by the time of this book's publication, the Cashmere School District was and continues to be academically ambitious, athletically vigorous, and artistically excellent. Since the days of the Frances Willard High School, named in honor of the turn-of-the-century founder of the Woman's Christian Temperance Union, Cashmere School District No. 222 has been recognized as having an "outstanding record of academic and athletic achievement," to quote Laura Arksey of HistoryLink.

The Cashmere High School football team is an exemplar of the school system's organizational pride. Until the 1990s, the team heralded its regular victories on the field with a man-sized, propane-fired cannon that was shot off after every touchdown. Many locals fondly, and some not so fondly, remember the report of this overgrown potato gun, which could be heard for miles on every game night and now sits in the storefront of Brian's Bulldog Pizza on Cottage Avenue.

Cashmere's schools are equally well known for their arts and music programs. The author's older brother Steven, for instance, went with Cashmere's brainy Knowledge Bowl team on the road across central Washington, helping the high school team defeat many of the region's best and brightest. Then, under the beloved husband-and-wife team of David and Priscilla Baldock during the 1990s, Cashmere musicians marched in parades in Canada, sang in state competitions, took first place at the New Orleans Jazz Festival (the author's younger brother, Eric, playing lead alto saxophone), and routinely won regional solo and ensemble contests.

Still, Cashmere never became a large town. Even with its increase in wealth, it has barely grown in population since it dropped the name Mission. The estimated population within city limits in 1906 was 450, and by 1920 the total was a mere 1,114. This trend continued into the next millennium, with the 2010 census revealing a population of 3,063, just over two and a half times what it had been 90 years earlier.

There has been some growth worth mentioning, namely migrant Mexican laborers and their second-generation American children. Sometimes living in tension with the earlier population, the primarily Spanish-speaking *migrantes* have nevertheless steadily assimilated into Cashmere and jointly written its history. In spite of the cultural friction, immigration is nothing new to rural Washington. In fact, the flow of contemporary foreigners continues Cashmere's long history of successful immigration, like that of the Armenian-born Armen Tersagian and Mark Balaban, who founded Liberty Orchards, and the German-born Alexander Brender. One such modern-day immigrant is the Mexican-born "Juan," whose true name I have withheld at his request.

Juan, like so many Mexicans who live in what is today Cashmere, is an American success story. A man of deep Catholic convictions, he fled the poverty and failed politics of his native country for the hope of a stable and prosperous life. Paying human traffickers known as "coyotes," Juan was the first of his family to come across, establishing himself as a hired hand at a local orchard. Earning the respect of the owner, and a steady paycheck, he saved enough to bring his wife and immediate relatives to America. Though they are not proud to have flouted immigration laws to come here, and insist they would have done otherwise if they could, Juan and his family are nevertheless proud of the entrepreneurial spirit that has led them to be successful business owners and to raise thoroughly loyal, decent, American children. Juan represents the best of that same spirit that brought the author's own German relative, Alexander, here a century and a half ago.

Shown here is a c. 1925 Sim Drug Company postcard of Cashmere. The Sim drug store was a competitor of the Cashmere drug store, which occupied a space directly across from it on Cottage Avenue. The view in this photograph looks southeast, following the Wenatchee River's course to the Columbia 10 miles away. Featured on the right are the Wenatchee River footbridge and, in the distance, the paved Cottage Avenue Bridge. This photograph was taken by L.B. Waters and originally published by the Sim Drug Company.

This image is formed from a five-part collection of postcards sold around 1913. This panorama looks down on Cashmere, then nine years old, from "Number Hill," so called for the seniors of the Cashmere School District painting their graduation year on it. In the early 1900s, it was a

common marketing scheme to break up sweeping panoramas of places into multiple postcards, which were meant to be collected and displayed together.

This picture is facing north along Division Street toward Number Hill (the prominent terrain feature that was later restyled "Letter Hill") around 1945. The rock edifice at lower right has two man-sized alcoves that recess only a few feet; however, imaginative Cashmere children have long fancied that they led into the heart of the hill overlooking the eastern end of town.

The view in this c. 1915 photograph looks southwest toward Division Street, which is clearly visible running from center to upper left. One third of the way up the hill in the background is a dark horizontal line. This is the Icicle Irrigation Ditch, built approximately 15 years earlier, which still supplies agricultural water to the naturally semiarid valley. This photograph was published by Rohen Photo of Billings, Montana.

Cottage Avenue Park, which is located close to the Wenatchee River, is shown here in 1936. E.C. Long willed .76 acres of his orchard to the City of Cashmere on the condition that the land be used as a public park. During the 1920s and 1930s, the space had a bandstand gazebo that held weekly open-air concerts.

Cashmere, Washington
Shortly after construction of the North Division Street Bridge in 1957. Original Photo by Ellis.

Shown here is a northeasterly view of Cashmere from the ridgelines south of town in 1957. This picture was taken by local pharmacist Ben Ellis shortly after the construction of the North Division Street Bridge. Ellis was the successor to pharmacist Ron "Mr. Cashmere" Doane, for whom the Cashmere High School gymnasium is named. Ellis has made pictorial calendars from his own scenic photographs of the central Washington area every year from the early 1950s to the present.

This is a 1906 view of Cashmere and the Wenatchee River looking east. The black line at center is a passenger train headed west, bound for the treacherous Stevens Pass and distant Seattle. This very mountain railway line would later be the subject of the infamous Wellington Disaster, which claimed 96 lives in 1910 and is still the worst train accident in US history.

Here is a 1930s photograph of Cottage Avenue facing west from the bridge spanning the Wenatchee River. The bridge is only a few yards downstream from the former location of Big Rock, the popular local swimming site.

This is a 1908 panorama of Cashmere facing west. At the bottom, on the near side of the Wenatchee River, is Smith's Grove. The Smith family frequently hosted Indian families on their land and later donated it to the City of Cashmere on the condition that it be used for public recreation. The part of this area to the left of Cottage Avenue, the vertical road at center, is the modern-day site of the Cashmere Museum. The right side is now private property, including the house of Christ Center pastor Steven Haney.

Here is a view south along Division Street. Note the paucity of trees in that part of town compared to the modern day, a testament to the waterless conditions of the valley in its natural state. In 1906, elms and poplar trees were planted along the roadways; many of them still stand today.

Cottage Avenue is shown here in the summer of 1936. Now verdant with trees after 26 years of growth, Cashmere continued to cultivate its sylvan heritage during the 20th century, and in 1986 was granted membership in the Arbor Day Foundation's Tree City USA registry. Many of the houses seen here still exist, including the one on the far right with the arch-shaped entryways.

Prominent in this c. 1935 west-facing photograph's foreground is Cottage Avenue, and at center in the background is Stine's Hill, also known as Needlepoint. This terrain feature's second name is derived from the wildflowers growing on it, which resemble a work of needlepoint embroidery. Interestingly, this photograph's caption describes the roadway as part of the "Yellowstone Trail." Though that name and knowledge of its origin have not survived to modern times, it is likely that it is was called this because Highway 2 runs east to Wyoming, passing somewhat near Yellowstone National Park.

This view looking west is near the present-day Cashmere Museum. It shows the Cottage Avenue bridge at left and a second bridge on the right that went to a small island in the Wenatchee River. Neither the island nor the bridge on the right exist today. The island was excavated from the river during the construction of Highway 2 and used to reinforce the flood-prone banks of the Wenatchee River in 1958.

This is a postcard of the Cashmere Train Depot published in the early 1900s. The depot was iconic even then, and this artifact of rail travel in the Northwest was published by a printing company in far-off West Bethel, Maine. The roofline that shows just above the left end of the depot is the two-story frame structure that housed the Cashmere Post Office until 1912.

In December 2018, the *Wenatchee World* ran this picture of the Cashmere Hotel, the first inn to directly cater to passengers on the all-important railway. Later renamed the Blewett Hotel, it stood at the corner of Division and Mission Streets. It was built in 1905 and its original name reflects the town's then brand-new one. The hotel went through a string of owners during its life, including George Baily and Myrtle Fasken, Nina Fish, Mr. and Mrs. Arthur MacPherson, and Mr. and Mrs. Herbert Lentz. In the mid-1960s, as rail travel became more passé, the space was converted to a Greyhound bus station under the management of Aurelia Brisky and remained in operation until its demolition in 1976. (Courtesy of the *Wenatchee World*.)

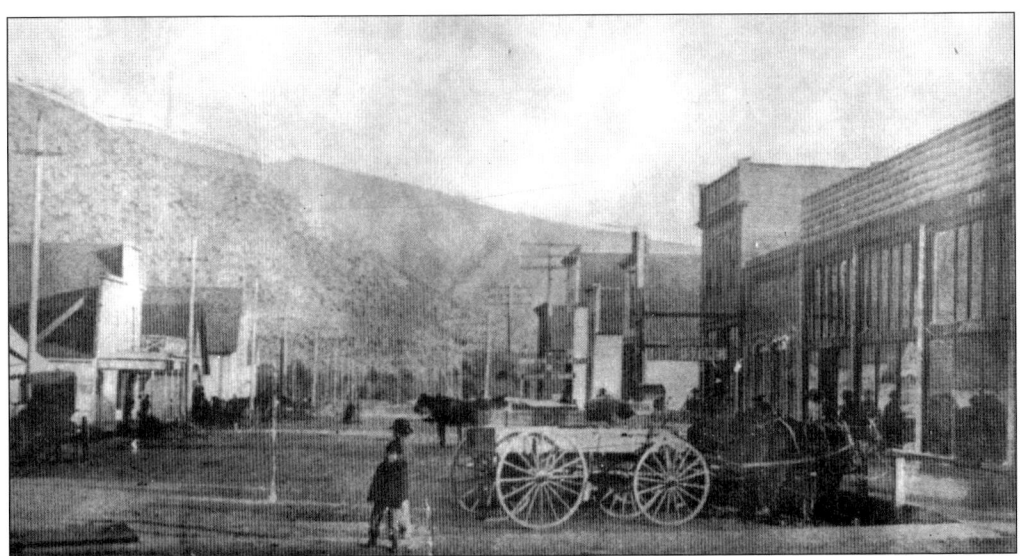

Downtown Cashmere is shown here in 1908. Taken from the future site of the Cashmere Valley Bank, this view looks east along what became Cottage Avenue toward Letter Hill, upon which high school seniors renovated the giant "C" annually in lieu of the former practice of painting the high school class's graduating year.

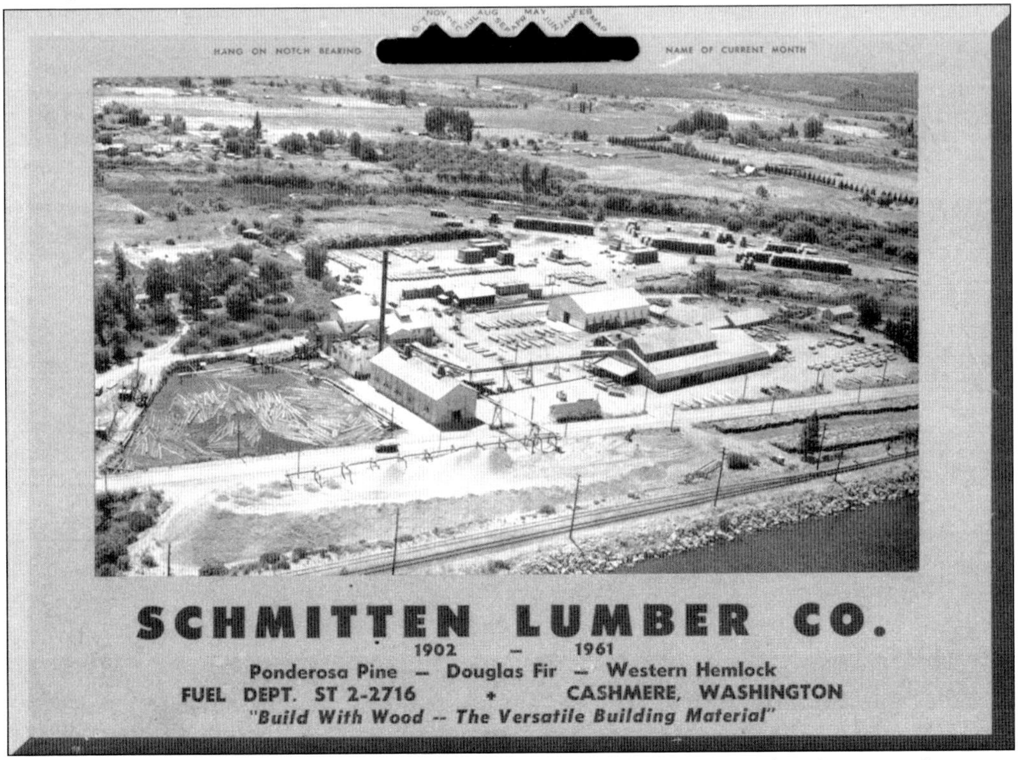
HANG ON NOTCH BEARING
NAME OF CURRENT MONTH
SCHMITTEN LUMBER CO.
1902 – 1961
Ponderosa Pine — Douglas Fir — Western Hemlock
FUEL DEPT. ST 2-2716 • CASHMERE, WASHINGTON
"Build With Wood -- The Versatile Building Material"

This is the backing of a promotional calendar from the Schmitten Lumber Company featuring its second mill, which was located along Highway 2 near the Goodwin Bridge and was lost to a fire in 2006. The facility lay in ruins until cleanup operations began in 2017. (Courtesy of the Schmitten Lumber Company)

Shown here is the Cashmere Post Office at its Grange location on Cottage Avenue and Woodring Street, then under the leadership of Cashmere's postmaster, Walter Olive (owner of the hardware store formerly colocated with the post office). In 1938, postal operations moved to the Haug Building, which was a subdivision of the present-day Cashmere Valley Bank, and then moved again to its present location at the corner of Elberta Avenue and Woodring Street in 1959. The names of the individuals in this c. 1929 photograph are not known, but notice the dark forearm bands the man in the middle is wearing. These armbands were used to protect postal workers' shirts from wet ink.

The Cashmere J.C. Penney department store was built in 1929 and closed in 1965. The inscription on the back of this photograph, written by an unidentified employee, reads, "1949–1950 I had the baby dept. & ladies ready to wear." In a second hand, the inscription continues, "Mr Andrews was the manager." From 1965 to 1967, it was Edward's Department Store, and from 1967 to 1969 Fred Holland, one of the last managers of the department store, leased the building and converted it into the Upper Valley Department Store.

This is another photograph of the Cashmere J.C. Penney, taken during the same period. Notice the sign on the right for "oil cloth," an early type of waterproof material. After the space's incarnation as the Upper Valley Department Store, it became Cashmere Drug until 1985, when it was a competitor to Sim Drugs and later Doane's Pharmacy, only the last of which has survived to the modern day.

This view looks west along Cottage Avenue sometime between 1938, when the Vale Theater on the left was built in the Grange Building, and 1952, when the Modowmoor Dairy, on the far right, was torn down to make way for Leo Cope's Mobiloil station.

FARMERS & MERCHANTS BANK - CASHMERE, WASH.   FIRST STATE BANK

Shown here are the Farmers & Merchants Bank (left) and the First State Bank (right). According to Cashmere historian Tom Hart in 2018, "The building that today houses Brian's Pizza was built in 1904 for the Farmers & Merchants Bank. The Cashmere State Bank was started in a lean-to building just east of the present Clifford's Hardware building. The Cashmere State Bank built the building on the right in 1909. Not to be outdone, the Farmers & Merchants Bank built the building on the left in 1909 or 1910, a little bit bigger, a little bit taller, a little bit fancier." Farmers & Merchants Bank was bought out by Cashmere State Bank in 1931. The merger failed in early 1932. The First State Bank became the Cashmere Valley Bank on September 24, 1932, when brothers H.H. Rieke and Hy W. Rieke paid for the latter by selling their interest in an Odessa, Washington, bank. The Cashmere Valley Bank filled the void left by the failure of all other financial institutions in Cashmere during the Great Depression.

For nearly 35 years, the Cashmere office was the only branch of the Cashmere Valley Bank. After the mid-1970s, however, the bank expanded dramatically to a total of nine satellite branches as far flung as Yakima and Bellevue, Washington.

Cashmere
Circa Early 1900's
9505094

From left to right in this 1908 photograph are the Big D Department Store, Homer Faust's Bakery, the Farmers & Merchants Bank, and Foust's Barber Shop. This photograph was originally published in the *Cashmere Valley Record*.

This is John Miller's Meat Market in 1905, which was located in downtown Cashmere in the vicinity of Cottage Avenue and Division Street. From left to right are Bill Lessinger, Charles "Chas." Blotti, Johnnie Miller, and Bill Towne.

The Richfield auto supply store and George's Tire Service, which once stood at the corner of Cottage Avenue and Division Street, are seen here. At the time of this photograph, cars still used carburetors to oxygenate their fuel mixture and inner tubes to hold air in their tires.

CASHMERE, WASH.

According to Cashmere historian Tom Hart, the Ellis Ford Department Store was built in 1907 and was "a very large building for that time—127 feet on Division Street, and 88 feet on Cottage Avenue. A fire in 1915 destroyed most of the Cottage Avenue side of the building. The northwest corner of the building was never rebuilt." The space later hosted the Cashmere Tire Company and a succession of filling stations until 1966, when it became the Ardeta Park.

Police Marshal Carlos E. "Spec" Johnston, who was born in 1907 in Asawatoomie, Kansas, served as the last constable of Cashmere. He moved to Monitor, Washington, about five miles southeast of Cashmere, and while there married Joesephina Cenory of Everett, Washington. In 1950, the couple resettled in Cashmere, where, after his service as constable, he worked at the Schmitten Mill until his death in 1962. Cashmere phased out its police department under Chief Alvin Whitten in the 1980s, leaving the town's law enforcement to the Chelan County Sheriff's Office.

The Potlatch Lumber Company burned to the ground on May 23, 1946, though its office (one of the former sites of the Cashmere Post Office) survived the blaze. In the foreground are the Cashmere Baptist Church and the M&M Chevrolet dealership. The dealership has since been demolished, but the Baptist church remains in active use.

This picture shows the destruction of the Potlatch Lumber Company as seen from near the railroad. *Potlatch* is a Chinook word that refers to a celebration where guests exchange gifts; it is often confused with a "potluck" by those unfamiliar with Pacific Northwest culture. Potlatch, along with other Salish words like *skookum* (good, big, manly), *hi-yup* (good friend) and *-chuck* (a suffix meaning stream), are regional words in use in the Pacific Northwest and southern British Columbia.

Here is another view of the Potlach Lumber Company fire. The Chevron station at center once stood to the left of the Cashmere Baptist Church, the south wall of which is visible at right.

This photograph, showing the view to the north side of the Cashmere Baptist Church, is a final look at the Potlatch Lumber Company fire. Always made of stern stuff, the Cashmere residents in the foreground seem remarkably unfazed by the uncontained fire burning directly behind two filling stations.

The facade of the Cashmere Baptist Church is shown here with its Attic columns. It was constructed in 1911 and still stands nearly unchanged in 2019. It is among Cashmere's earliest structures and was one of the few built with comparatively expensive bricks. The right side of this building is visible at left in the preceding Potlatch fire picture.

This Sim Drug Company postcard of downtown Cashmere was taken sometime between 1912, when sidewalks and curbs were installed, and 1919, when the town's roadways were paved. While horseless carriages such as those in this picture eased the burdens of travel, their low speeds and the poor quality of highways still made even nearby cities like Wenatchee a significant trip. As such, early-20th-century Cashmere residents often had little choice but to buy local, encouraging the diversity of goods and service shops shown here.

The Cashmere Fire Department poses for a photograph in front of its station with its wagons sometime prior to the building's demolition in 1927. The structure is the original frame school building that was moved from Division Street to the corner of Mission and Woodring Streets in 1907 using rollers and teams of horses.

The prominent three-story building on the left is the old Cashmere Grange on Cottage Avenue. Although the 1912 three-story building still exists, it has been reduced in height. The top floor and back third of the building were removed when the Grange structure was condemned after several fires, leaving it vacant from 1955 to 1960 until the space was converted to the Evergreen Restaurant. Throughout its storied history, the Grange Building has been home to over 40 businesses and service organizations.

Beginning in the 1940s, Kelly Tosch (far right) owned and operated the Cashmere Tire Shop for 17 years before selling it to K. McGee of Chelan. Pictured with Kelly are Vernon Broaddus and Arthur Tosch.

The Schmitten Lumber Company was one of the most influential early businesses in Cashmere. From the first record of it in 1905 until its sale to Carl Stevens in 1945, it kept 80 employees, had a payroll of over $100,000, sold 10 million board feet of lumber, and produced 800,000 apple boxes annually. At the time of this photograph, the Schmitten retail lumberyard (at 206 Woodring Street, the present location of a seniors' apartment building), was owned by the Schmitten estate and managed by W.W. Jones.

This photograph originally appeared in a *Cashmere Valley Record* advertisement for the Columbia Lumber Company, formerly the Columbia Valley Lumber Company and later the Sunset Land Agency. The text accompanying the image features an interesting eastern Washington regional phrase. The ad boasts that the business carried a full line of locally sourced materials that otherwise could only be purchased "on the coast." Locally, "the coast" refers to any city along Puget Sound, a large, sheltered bay that is far removed from the actual ocean coastline. Ironically, actual coastal cities like Hoquiam and Aberdeen are not generally included in many eastern Washingtonians' estimation of "the coast."

Charlie Clements (left) was the owner of Skookum Service, which he boasted, perhaps untruthfully, was the first service station in Cashmere. The caption for this photograph, from a 1975 *Cashmere Valley Record* article, indicates that Skookum Service was located at "the site of the present Mobil station on Cottage Avenue." Notice the gasoline pumps; in 1925, when this picture was taken, gasoline was pumped into one-gallon glass tops so that the customer could verify the volume and then manually released into the fueling hose. Francis Sullivan is the man on the right, standing in front of a poster that the original article noted advertised the Leavenworth District Fair.

This is an undated, though clearly early-20th-century photograph of downtown Cashmere along Cottage Avenue, with a view of the valley's commanding hills to the northeast.

Washington, like the rest of the Pacific Northwest, benefits from hydroelectric power. The nearest hydroelectric plant to Cashmere is the Rocky Reach Dam in Wenatchee, pictured here on October 19, 1960. Thanks to the Columbia River, electricity in north central Washington costs a fraction of what it does in other parts of the country, especially those areas fueled by coal.

The East Cashmere Market stood at the current location of the Antique Mall at Cashmere, directly across from the Rusty's Drive-In. The three employees in this photograph are unidentified.

Richard "Dick," or "Tiny," Graves was Cashmere's self-proclaimed "Cider King." Graves founded a small roadside fruit stand with his father's money in 1953 and grew it into a highway circus, putting up advertising signs as far away as Montana, California, and British Columbia. In her book *Tiny: King of the Roadside Vendors*, Sharon Graves Hall describes Dick, her older brother, as "a master showman . . . replete with bright, floral shirts clashing with plaid Bermuda shorts, and a crown (literally)." His business was a Cashmere fixture for two decades until he died in December 1971 at the age of 41. To compound this tragedy, his fruit stand burned to the ground six months after his passing. It was replaced with a smaller iteration of the business, under former partner Dan Slechta, which operated until November 1981, when that venture failed. Tiny's stand was located near the site of the current Martin's Market Place.

Fruit tree orcharding has been a mainstay of business in Cashmere since the town's early inception. In this photograph is a Red Delicious apple tree. Notice the abundance of young limbs, which implies that this photograph was taken prior to the widespread implementation of modern pruning and thinning around the 1930s. Pruning is the reduction of fruit-bearing branches, and thinning is the removal of a portion of young fruit growing on the tree, both of which help to eliminate bruising and lead to larger, more valuable apples.

This 1932 photograph shows "Mr Simpson . . . father of Wayne Simpson" and was mostly likely taken in Mission Creek, on the south end of Cashmere. Simpson's trees are in bloom, which means that this photograph was taken around April or May.

This undated photograph records the Richardson family. Even without words, one can glean an appreciation for the lifestyle early Cashmere residents lived. Despite the community's special emphasis on education and civic society, the hard work of agriculture was never far from anyone's mind. The adult in the back is George J. Richardson, and in front are his children, from left to right (and from youngest to oldest), Horace, Victor E., Norman E., Oscar P., Roy E., Lemiul (deceased by the time this print was inscribed), George H., Kellis J., Lefson (?) H., and Walter S. Not pictured are Philip E. Richardson, George's second-oldest son, who died in childhood; Alice (Richardson) Clark, his oldest daughter; and Elsie (Richardson) Bishop.

This orchardist is shaping his tree using the more modern method that limits its height. Preventing a tree from growing taller redirects nutrients to existing limbs and encourages fruit production at heights no greater than that of a typical 10-to-14-foot ladder.

S.P. Beecher lived to a ripe age in the upper Wenatchee Valley and was previously depicted in this book in chapter two, about 55 years before this summer 1955 picture was taken. Here, the 83-year-old Beecher operates a bulldozer on his Mountain Home property, on the ridgeline overlooking the southern edge of Leavenworth.

Tree fruit has been the heart of the Cashmere economy since 1883, when D.S. Farrar, a hay grower who had arrived only the previous year, planted his first fruit tree in town. Today, apples, pears, and cherries account for the lion's share of agricultural production in the valley, including these apples from Liberty Orchards. Notice the shafts of wood in this late summer image: these are props, which field hands use to support heavily laden branches, preventing the limbs from being ripped off under their own weight as the fruit matures. (Courtesy of Liberty Orchards.)

93

A Cashmere fruit tree is shown here likely in the earliest stages of spring. Its branches are bare except for a single brown leaf at upper center. All fruit trees in the area are dormant during the intensely cold winter months, only budding as the ambient temperature rises and daylight duration increases. This tree reflects an older style of training, or shaping. The owner of this orchard has placed a guy wire to set the tree in a "formal upright" position, ostensibly hoping to produce a greater yield or a longer lifespan. As of 2019, most trees are trimmed to be lower and wider, speeding the picking process without lessening quantity or quality. (Courtesy of Liberty Orchards.)

A Liberty Orchards grower is shown here mowing his land. The tractor he is riding powers the mower by means of the exposed drive shaft, the upper of the two metal pieces extending from beneath the driver's seat. The drive shaft turns the gearbox shown in the center of the mower, which powers large spinning blades sometimes a yard across to quickly make orchards clean and easy to maintain. The tractor is unusual by 21st-century standards in that it is tracked instead of wheeled. Tracked vehicles are superior on extremely soft ground, such as is often found in orchards, because they more equally distribute the weight of the vehicle across the ground, preventing miring. Unlike wheeled tractors, which steer by angling their front tires left or right, tracked vehicles slow one side's rotation relative to the other, causing the vehicle to pivot. (Courtesy of Liberty Orchards.)

The Red Delicious is perhaps the most widely recognizable variety of apple in the world. It is an example of a dessert apple, one that is sweet and textured enough to eat on its own. (Courtesy of Liberty Orchards.)

GRADING APPLES · CASHMERE · WASH

Local women are shown grading apples after they have been brought from storage. Apples are categorized by size according to how many fit into a one-bushel box, which measures 11 inches by 11 inches by 18 inches, and then graded by numerous factors including color, skin clarity, and damage. Damaged fruit are known as culls and are usually relegated to being juiced.

This picture captures the fruit-growing practice of spraying, the application of pesticides or inert substances, such as clay, to trees in order to prevent insect infestations and infections. Fire blight is one such destructive bacterial infection. Spread by wind, pollinators, or infected pruning tools, fire blight can destroy an entire orchard's crop. (Courtesy of Liberty Orchards.)

In this January 1954 photograph is Marvin Joseph "Red" Brouillette, a fieldman for the Cashmere Pioneer Growers. A fieldman was a warehouse advisor in charge of helping contracted orchardists produce the greatest harvest for the company. He directed his growers in the method and timing of applying insecticides, pruning, tree care, planting, and other issues that affected the ability of orchardists to bring their best yield to market. A US Marine Corps field artillery officer in the Second World War, he earned his nickname for his hair, which was reportedly striking in his youth. (Courtesy of Joseph Brouillette.)

Early in a fruit tree's development, growers desire leaders, the tree limbs off of which lateral growths develop. Lateral growths are the younger, more flexible shoots from which fruit buds develop. Leaders that are too horizontal produce excess lateral growth, robbing individual fruit of the tree's finite quantity of sap, and leaders that are at an angle greater than 45 degrees encourage terminal growth, the overall length of a limb, which again diverts sap away from fruit production in favor of the limb itself. Red Brouillette is inspecting for proper leader development. (Courtesy of Joseph Brouillette.)

Armen Tertsagian (left) and Mark Balaban (right) founded the candy company Liberty Orchards, creating the famous confection Aplets & Cotlets based on their native Armenia's *locum*. Thanks to C.S. Lewis's *The Chronicles of Narnia*, locum is perhaps best known to the world as Turkish delight. Soon after the turn of the 20th century, the young Tertsagian immigrated to the United States, working his way from Ellis Island to Seattle. There he met Balaban, another young Armenian, who was visiting from England. The two became friends and business partners. Their initial ventures, a yogurt factory and an Armenian restaurant, were ahead of their time, and the weather was difficult for people used to a Mediterranean climate. Tertsagian and Balaban moved to eastern Washington, settling in the Vale of Cashmere, where they purchased an apple farm, which they named Liberty Orchards in honor of their new homeland.

According to David Simmer of Liberty Orchards, this is the oldest known photograph of Aplets & Cotlets operations. It was likely taken in the early 1920s and shows a belt-operated machine, perhaps a candy cutter, which the woman on the left was apparently not tall enough to operate on her own. These were humble beginnings for a company whose 21st-century chief executive officer, Greg Taylor, is a Harvard Business School graduate. (Courtesy of Liberty Orchards.)

This steel kettle was the very first cooking vessel in which Aplets were commercially made. Its two- or three-gallon capacity is dwarfed by the massive vats that today produce several tons of Aplets & Cotlets. (Courtesy of Liberty Orchards.)

Aplets Packers at Work
Aplets Factory, Cashmere, Wash.

This image of Aplets & Cotlets factory workers was taken by prolific local photographer A.G. Simmer. At lower left, beneath the Simmer Studio brand mark, is a four-digit number, 1856. This is the original print's serial number. Simmer catalogued every photograph that he developed and embossed each print, including postcards, with his personal serial number. (Courtesy of Liberty Orchards.)

Ed Winterton (left) and Elmer Presler pour walnuts into the hot liquid Aplets & Cotlets base as it begins the cooling process. (Courtesy of Liberty Orchards.)

Tom Hendrickson, still employed at Aplets & Cotlets at the time of this book's publication, stirs the heated, sugary base of the candy in a steel drum. Though made in large quantities, Aplets & Cotlets are still batched in drums just like the ones shown here. (Courtesy of Liberty Orchards.)

Ezra Meeker, at the time of this photograph one of the oldest surviving forefathers of Cashmere, is being treated to Aplets & Cotlets by the workers who made and packaged them. Before the age of automation, each piece was individually wrapped and placed within a paper sleeve in its box. (Courtesy of Liberty Orchards.)

The Aplets & Cotlets factory in downtown Cashmere is one of the oldest continuously operating businesses in the valley. The making of the candy itself is a labor-intensive process equaled only by the amount of work involved in its packaging, even with the benefit of modern machinery. Often, Cashmere's young women have performed this latter task, including the one at front left in this 1928 image, whose name is unfortunately lost to history. (Courtesy of Liberty Orchards.)

Likely taken in the late fall, this 1928 photograph shows the assembly line workers of Aplets & Cotlets, which is still headquartered at the same location on Mission Street as it was in 1918. (Courtesy of Liberty Orchards.)

Richard Odabashian, a World War II pilot who continued flying after leaving the service, was Liberty Orchards' "Mr. Outside." Aplets & Cotlets marketing director David Simmer (no known relation to the local photographer A.G. Simmer) said in 2018 that Odabashian was famous in his lifetime for his elaborate marketing campaigns, typically involving his personal aeronautics. Later marrying into the family of Liberty Orchards cofounder Mark Balaban, Odabashian teamed up with John Chakirian (Balaban's nephew) to lead the company. (Courtesy of Liberty Orchards.)

A venerable Cashmere resident places Aplets & Cotlets into her tray with studied precision. Considering the apparently plastic trays she is using, as opposed to the company's original individual paper cups, this picture was likely taken no earlier than the 1950s. The clock at upper left tells us that it is about 3:25 p.m., meaning she probably is keenly aware that she only has about an hour and a half until she can go home from her eight-hour shift. (Courtesy of Liberty Orchards.)

Though operations have grown considerably since its inception, this perhaps 1960s-era picture shows the Liberty Orchards retail office. The modern-day shop, as in this photograph, retains a remarkably intimate ambiance with candies, local mustards, and handmade gifts. Notice the original Aplets cooking kettle in the lower right of the display case. (Courtesy of Liberty Orchards.)

This 1929 A.G. Simmer photograph is possibly the most iconic and most reproduced image of the Cashmere Valley. It shows a view west toward Mount Cashmere in late spring. Views like this are annual occurrences in Cashmere, with the mountain snows lasting well into summer. Several things in this picture persist into the modern era. On the hillside to the lower left of Mount Cashmere, the dark horizontal line is the Peshastin Ditch, which has provided local orchards with water for nearly 100 years. The tall poplar trees at center are some of those first planted in 1906, which still stand. (Courtesy of Liberty Orchards.)

This image of the Liberty Orchards fields was taken in Cashmere prior to the company selling them off in the 1950s. The young women were factory line workers posing for a Liberty Orchards marketing campaign.

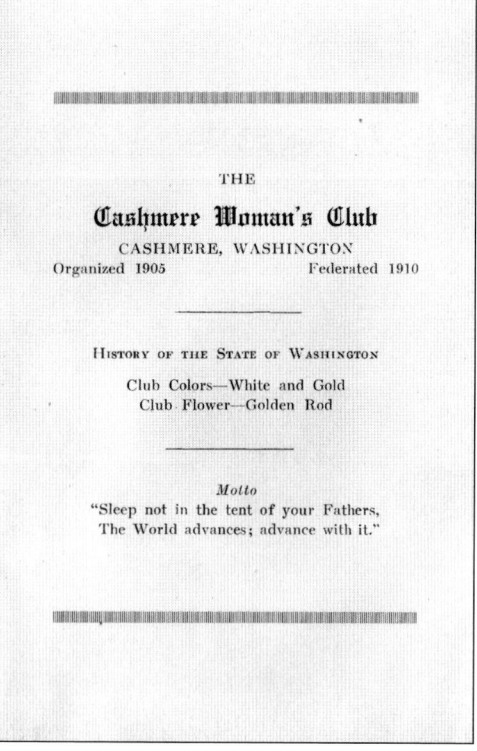

THE

Cashmere Woman's Club

CASHMERE, WASHINGTON

Organized 1905   Federated 1910

HISTORY OF THE STATE OF WASHINGTON

Club Colors—White and Gold
Club Flower—Golden Rod

Motto
"Sleep not in the tent of your Fathers,
The World advances; advance with it."

The Cashmere Woman's Club was known from 1906 to 1913 as the Minerva Club. Cashmere, though a pioneer town, was a generally peaceful settlement that did not have the bawdy character of neighboring Leavenworth, then famous as a rough-hewn train town. Organizations like the Rotary, the American Legion, and the Boy Scouts were prominent in Cashmere from its earliest days.

Shown here are Fred Abeling (left) and Otto "Ott" Brender tending a horse around 1906, with Nahahum Canyon in the background. Otto was the first cousin, one generation removed from Alexander Bartolomäus Brender, and the son of Frederick Leonard Brender and Emma Miller. He was born in Eudora, Kansas, in 1891. After his family relocated to nearby Leavenworth at Alexander's invitation, he married Estella L. Hughes and the couple had one daughter, Elisabeth. Otto lived to be 100 years old before passing away in Freeland, Washington, on Whidbey Island.

Warehouse magnate and friend to the Wenatchi Willis Carey dives into a hole in search of a "whistle jack," also known as a hoary marmot. The reverse of this print identifies the man holding his feet as his friend Earl Wohlers, for whom a road near the mouth of Brender Canyon is named. In addition to his business savvy and Indian relationships, Carey is also famous for being an adventurous outdoorsman and for serving as Chelan County's first game warden. Still, he is best known for his donation of Indian artifacts to the City of Cashmere on the condition it properly display them. The city agreed to these terms, even going so far as to originally name that display the Willis Carey Museum.

This undated picture shows, from left to right, Tom Parrish, Paddy Paton, Bill Dooley, Clarence Jack, and Earl Wohlers, most likely in The Enchantments, a portion of the Cascade Range near Leavenworth. Judging by the professional quality of the photograph, these men put considerable effort into their trips and likely invited along a skilled photographer.

Also likely in the Cascade's Enchantments, from left to right, are "Packer," Clarence Jack, Paddy Paton, Tom Parrish, and Earl Wohlers.

Undated and with no location given, though maybe from the same expedition as the images on the previous page, this photograph shows, from left to right, Bill Dooley, Clarence Jack, Tom Speller, "Tacker" (perhaps the same man as the earlier mentioned "Packer"), Tom Parrish, and Earl Wohlers.

Also undated, this photograph's back side reads, "Tom Speller shimming a log across the Chockalit Creek. Could hear boulders rolling on bottom." The body of water Speller is crawling over is perhaps a high Cascade tributary of the Wenatchee or Icicle Rivers, which converge in Leavenworth and flow through Cashmere to the mighty Columbia.

Earl Wohlers and Clarence Jack are pictured hunting in Montana. Text on the back of the original print places them in Buck Creek, a location that afforded them a magnificent view of Glacier Peak in the background.

A c. 1935 article in the *Cashmere Valley Record* features John Marshall, an early Scottish immigrant to town. Marshall traveled throughout America for five years before settling in Cashmere and said "if I hadn't already ordered my equipment for a shoe repair shop I would have left Cashmere that first day. It was the 24th day of March [1908] and the wind was blowing so much dust you couldn't see across the street." The article goes on to state that Marshall was further disgusted by the ribald caterwauling of a charivari, a noisy, mock serenade that locals sang in honor of the newly wedded Mr. and Mrs. Guy Long, which was a sight the Scotsman found most appalling. However, Marshall's long tenure in town implies he found a way to make peace with both the town's weather and its revelers. He relinquished his 30-year ownership of the then-oldest continuously operating business in town, a shoe repair shop, to C.L. Starr in 1938.

This 1939 picture, featured in the *Cashmere Valley Record*, shows the "Cashmere Pioneers." German immigrant Alexander Bartolomäus Brender is fifth from the right in the front row. The others, from left to right, are (first row) John Kuelbs, Grant Paton, Fred Slauson, Mrs. W. Lawrence, Alexander Brender, Lou Titchenel (likely the man Titchenal Road near modern-day Martin's Market Place is named after), Dandy Bills, Tom Henry, A.C. Jones, Walter Moore, and George Lessenger; (second row) Sam Reid, Bill McPherson, Chester Clark, Jack Angier, Otis Rank, John Francisco, Al Holtzhouser, and A.H. Mohler; (third row) Jim Mortimer, George Noeker, Charles Ferrel, Charles Joy, Fred Abeling, Margaret Williams, and Mrs. A.H. Mohler; (fourth row) E.J. Uecker, Perry Bixler, Mel Erickson, Tom Hudson, Cora Charlton, Mrs. Chapell, Mrs. Ern Searles, and Mrs. W.H. Lawrence; (fifth row) Guy Long (to whose charivari Scottish immigrant John Marshall took such a disliking), George Fasken, Herbert Remley, Clark Bixler, Fred Mintzer, S.H. Miller, Ben Vaughn, and Ern Searles.

LuEva Jones, daughter of A.C. Jones (the first mayor of Mission) and Jessie (Bell) Jones, is pictured here with the Wenatchee River and Nahahum Canyon in the background around 1910.

The Vernon, British Columbia, Girls' Drill Team is shown here entertaining the crowd during what the *Cashmere Valley Record* called "this year's barbecue dinner" on Cottage Avenue. The view looks east from the vicinity of the Cashmere Valley Bank sometime after 1978.

This is an undated photograph of the Cashmere marching band. The marching band was a municipal group, unaffiliated with the school, even though Cashmere High School is clearly visible in the background. The photograph's inscription lists Chas Kuelbs in the front row and Wilson Amos in the second, with C.A. Doyle and Mel Bourne also in the image.

Taken sometime prior to 1956, when the county fair was still held in Leavenworth, this photograph shows the westernmost extent of what became the Chelan County Fairgrounds. The houses on the left are the current staging area west of the rodeo field, and the gravel pile on the right is in the general location of the fairgrounds' main entrance. In 1956, local Charlie Clements lobbied Chelan County to appropriate funds for the development of the fairgrounds in Cashmere. This move met with fierce opposition from a Wenatchee group, the Applettes, who unsuccessfully counter-petitioned to have the fair moved to Wenatchee, the county seat. (Courtesy of Jim and Janet Flagel.)

In this view looking east, the lowlands in the midground are what is now the Chelan County Fairgrounds parking lot. Prior to the early 1970s, however, that area was the King Brothers concrete plant, one of the last industrial facilities in Cashmere. (Courtesy of Jim and Janet Flagel.)

Jim Flagel, longtime supporter of the Chelan County Fair, took this aerial photograph as he was building the Dawn Lee Courts housing development. Dawn Lee would later occupy the upper right section of the land pictured, above Kimber Road. The fairground dirt horseracing track is clearly visible at bottom right; racing continued in Cashmere until the 1970s, when a jockey died after being thrown from his horse. (Courtesy of Jim and Janet Flagel)

Jim Flagel (left) and a teenager from his church are repurposing trusses from the demolished 1952 Chelan County Fairgrounds cattle barn into a garage in 1998. Flagel has served as the unofficial historian of the fairgrounds since its inception. (Courtesy of Jim and Janet Flagel.)

In the back seat are Clyde Pangborn (right) and Hugh Herndon Jr. on parade in Wenatchee. Pangborn and Herndon were pilot and copilot, respectively, of the first nonstop flight from Japan to the United States. Taking off from Misawa, Japan, their Bellanca Skyrocket, the *Miss Veedol*, landed on Fancher Field in what is now East Wenatchee in 1931. In order to save weight and fuel, the crew ditched their landing gear shortly after takeoff, planning to make a "belly landing" on American soil. The automobile they are riding in was provided by the Cashmere Ford dealership.

This plane crashed near the mouth of Brender Canyon around the late 1950s. The pilot was a man by the last name of Moss, who left behind at least one orphaned son, Paul. Flight through the canyons around Cashmere is particularly dangerous because of the boxed-in airspace created by the hills and the perilously strong downdrafts. Still, the town is home to the Cashmere-Dryden Airport, which has been in operation since July 1950.

Ernest Tonk (1889–1968) was a painter renowned for his Western-themed works, often focusing on human subjects both posed and in dramatic action. In 1908, he met the famous "Buffalo Bill" Cody, who, impressed with the 19-year-old's work, became a strong guiding force for Tonk. Encouraged to travel westward, Tonk captured the vastness of America while he lived as a cowhand, wrangler, and logger, finally settling in Cashmere. Many of his paintings depict the majesty of the area. Later, at the age of 34, he accepted a commission to paint action scenes for film studios such as Universal Pictures, Warner Bros., 20th Century Fox, Columbia Pictures, and Metro-Goldwyn-Mayer, where he created scenes no doubt influenced by his time in the valley. Tonk retired from commercial art in the 1960s.

Walter Graham (1903–2000) was, like Tonk, an accomplished artist. He lived in Wenatchee, though many of his pieces now hang in the Cashmere Museum. For years, Graham ran a large art gallery in Chicago, supporting numerous artistic leagues, and later became a charter member of the Washington State Arts Commission. Like so many today, he escaped the din of the city for the unpretentious beauty of rural life in the 1970s and served four years as the president of the North Central Washington Museum. With work more ethereal in form than Tonk, whose sharp realism serves perhaps as much as his hallmark as does his Western subject matter, Graham avoided unnecessary detail and instead created images that seem like memories rendered onto canvas, often capturing a feeling of great space and grandeur.

Shown here is an Apple Days celebration at the Cashmere Museum & Pioneer Village in the mid-1970s. Apple Days, known as Pioneer Days until just shortly before this picture was taken, is an annual celebration held the first weekend in October. Music, historical displays, and reenactments celebrate Cashmere's heritage.

Being in the Cascade Mountains' rain shadow, Cashmere receives comparatively little precipitation throughout the summer, just 14 inches versus the national average of 39 inches. What moisture it does see predominantly takes the form of snow, accumulating an average of 42 inches in a year, three more than the national mean.

In the days before Wenatchee and Leavenworth were easy to reach, local theaters, like the Vale in the background, were thriving businesses. The Blewett Hotel stands prominently in the foreground, occupying a location that was profitably convenient to rail passengers in the days of train travel. Note the white, arrow-shaped sign at far left that points the way to the "Aplets Plant."

The Cashmere Grange building's theater regularly hosted concerts and productions. This c. 1930s photograph shows the town's junior chorus.

Taken near the intersection of Division Street and Sunset Highway, this photograph shows a 1930s Vale Elementary class of students sitting on land that still belongs to the school today.

The names of the teacher and students in this early Cashmere photograph have been lost; however, the inscription on the back of the original states that this school building later became the town hall, and after that, the town fire station. That likely places this structure roughly where the Cashmere Valley Bank is today, not where the modern fire station is at the corner of Woodring Street and Cottage Avenue.

Junior and Senior Banquet. Cashmere High School Friday May 15, 1925. Photo by Lester A. Smith

This is the May 15, 1925, Cashmere High School junior and senior banquet. Cashmere school yearbooks have historically included the phrase "ka-hi-wa," which has long erroneously been thought to be a Wenatchi phrase. However, it is actually a shortening of "Kashmir High, Washington." This is a reference to the Vale of Kashmir in India, after which the town is named. This photograph was taken by Lester A. Smith.

Shown here is the 1938 faculty of Cashmere Junior High School, the predecessor to Cashmere Middle School. From left to right are (first row) Ina Currie, Wilma Hudleson, Naomi Posey, Helen Thompson, Ruth Rathbun, and Mary Scholer; (second row) Marshall Search, O.C. Woods, Wade Knisley, Fred Crosetto, and Ralph Peterson; (third row) Raymond Cronrath, Myron Ernst, V.B. Armstrong, and Ray V. Geise.

This is the graduation photograph of the Cashmere High School class of 1940. Notice that, unlike in the following photograph taken 29 years later, nearly every young man here is wearing a tie. The location of the high school at that time was on the southwest corner of Division Street and Sunset Avenue. This building was eventually retired when Cashmere's student population outgrew it.

Pictured on June 14, 1969, at the 30-year reunion of the Cashmere class of 1939 are, from left to right, (seated) Everett Watson, Herbert Goetz, Charlotte Snyder, Robert Virgin, Ross Jones, Leroy LaVigne, Lois (Vickery) Kaiser, Dale Vickery, and Don McKellar; (kneeling) Bertha Mewberry, Jackie (Ormsby) Smith, Dorothy (Hink) French, Melvin "Bud" Brender, Raymond "Bud" Schmitten, and Jim Uecker; (standing) Jim Caldwell, Bill Smith, Grace Truckenmiller, Bob Seidenstricker, Carl Brender, Katherine (Taber) Stavros, Duane Wilson, Warren Taber, Ernie Crothers, Marie Hanson, Jim Wilson, Melba Murdock, Mary Lou (LaVigne) Davis, Jay McManus, Bob Currie, Delbert Mikkelson, Earl Barnes, Lester King, and Harold Patterson.

1950 KA-HI-WA

BILL LIPPINCOTT

JERRY KENOYER
8

DICK BATES
11

ERNIE GARRETT
11

MILO FLAGEL
7

ALVIN BROWN
12

CLIFF CANNON
10

DON PEPIN
9

DWIGHT BOSTWICK
5

WALTER NELSON
14

ARTHUR GREIG
3

MARVIN SCHADLER
6

VERNON KIRBY
13

NINTH GRADE BASKETBALL

High school athletes in Cashmere have always held a place of honor in the community. While music, the performing arts, and academics all were taken very seriously even from its early days, the town's sports teams are its popular darlings. In addition to being participants in something that many adult residents had done themselves when young, Cashmere athletes have the notable benefit of often winning. District teams in football, baseball, basketball, and other sports regularly qualify for state championships and often take them (for instance, the Cashmere High School boys' basketball team won the state championship six times and placed at least third in an additional four seasons between 1971 and 2016). (Courtesy of Brian's Bulldog Pizza, Brian Wintermeier, Sara Takacs, and Stefan Miller.)

Cashmere High School Foot Ball Team 1924   Photo by Lester A. Smith

Football has been a beloved Cashmere pastime for nearly as long as organized schooling has existed. The 1924 Cashmere High School football team shown here predates today's padding and protective gear. In addition to the leather leggings these young men are wearing, players would have had a protective shirt and a padded leather helmet. Unfortunately, only four of these players' names were recorded on the reverse of the photograph: Joe Wiggins, Bob McClimons, ? Waters, ? Brooks, and ? Yanter.

W.M. Baxter, Coach.

Little is known about Cashmere School District baseball coach W.M. Baxter other than that he lived during the period when photographer A.G. Simmer was active, placing this picture likely in the 1930s. (Courtesy of Brian's Bulldog Pizza, Brian Wintermeier, Sara Takacs, and Stefan Miller.)

Exactly to whom Coach F.V. Magaurn inscribed this portrait is unknown. Regardless, Magaurn was probably a teacher within the district, and undoubtedly devoted many of his after-school hours to his team of student athletes. (Courtesy of Brian's Bulldog Pizza, Brian Wintermeier, Sara Takacs, and Stefan Miller.)

To my best all around ball play. F.V. Magaurn

Coach F.V. Magaurn

This is the 1920 Cashmere girls' basketball team. Though the names of these athletes are lost to time, the young women testify to the long history of sport and civic identity that typified Cashmere and set it apart from its neighbors Wenatchee, Monitor, Peshastin, Dryden (then Pine Flat), and Leavenworth. In more recent girls' basketball history, Cashmere High School junior Hailey Van Lith took a gold medal in the 2018 Youth Olympic Games and in the 2018 International Basketball Federation U17 World Cup, and was the 2018 USA Basketball three-on-three U18 National Championship most valuable player. (Courtesy of Brian's Bulldog Pizza, Brian Wintermeier, Sara Takacs, and Stefan Miller.)

Kneeling:
  Andy Robinson, Don Smith, Mark Smith, Byron Mustard, Walt Whitehall, Joe Brouillette, Burt Hoffman, Kelly McFall, Mgr.
Standing:
  Don Garrison, Ken Collins, Lee Stevenson, Bill Christman, Brian Stokes, Joel Clark, Keith Collins, George Makela, Coach.
Not Pictured: Dale Flick, Scott Olin.

This photograph shows the 1976–1977 Cashmere High School track team. Many of these individuals stayed in Cashmere, or left only to return home later in life. Several, like Don Smith and Walt Whitehall, went on to be teachers at the same school from which they graduated, and Ken Collins is today the assistant superintendent for the Lake Stevens School District in western Washington. Several others, including Andy Robinson and Joe Brouillette, went on to be clergy in the local Christ Center congregation. (Courtesy of Brian's Bulldog Pizza, Brian Wintermeier, Sara Takacs, and Stefan Miller.)

Reflecting a culture-oriented community, Cashmere High School once boasted its own small symphony orchestra, as shown in this 1922 photograph. Sadly, the Cashmere School District no longer has an orchestra, though it does have a concert band, a concert choir, a jazz band, and a jazz choir for students to perform in. (Courtesy of Garth Brender and the *Wenatchee World*.)

This 1941 Cashmere High School photograph shows the money, time, and devotion that the school and the local community poured into its music education program. This trend has continued through today, with students and former students performing at such prestigious venues as the New Orleans Jazz Festival in 2009, regional music competitions, and sporting events across the state. (Courtesy of Brian's Bulldog Pizza, Brian Wintermeier, Sara Takacs, and Stefan Miller.)

In this 1971 picture taken in Illinois, clockwise from top, Robert Slider, Cecil Gorey, David Wooten, and Dave Baldock ham it up for the camera. Dave and Priscilla Baldock led the Cashmere School District's music department for nearly a decade in the 1990s, earning a tremendously loyal following among the student body. The husband-and-wife team met at Wheaton College in Illinois and got married after he graduated. Dave's first job was in the Crete-Monee School District in Crete, Illinois. He taught elementary and middle school band under the supervision of Robert Slider, a highly respected director in the Midwest in the 1960s, 1970s, and 1980s. A year later, Priscilla was hired by the same school to teach choir and classroom music. In 1973, they relocated to New England to be closer to Priscilla's Connecticut family and again got jobs together in the Agawam School District in Massachusetts. Their two boys were born during the next several years. In 1981, they moved west to Wenatchee, and in 1983, Dave took over the band director position in the Cashmere School District. He followed Larry Johnson, a wonderful director at the high school, for many years. A year later, Priscilla got a part-time job at Vale Elementary teaching classroom music, a job that quickly grew to full-time middle and high school choir, again in the same building with her husband, Dave. In 1997, Dave led the band program at Wenatchee High School, and in 1999, Dave and Priscilla both took jobs in the Kent School District in Seattle's southern suburbs. Dave retired from his long career as an educator at Kentridge High School in the Seattle area in 2010. (Courtesy of David Baldock.)

PUBLIC SCHOOL, CASHMERE, WASH.

The original Cashmere High School, built in 1907, is shown here in the foreground on the left. Behind it is the Frances Willard School on Division Street, which was constructed four years prior. In 1906, the Willard School had an enrollment of 275 and was one of only two public three-story buildings ever erected in Cashmere, neither of which survived to the modern day. Interestingly, the Willard School's basement and first floor were built of rock, which caused the structure to sink into the soft ground until 1907, when it came to rest on firmer earth. With the structure still level, the school's administration simply added a second story of brick that same year. The now slightly taller school was named after the founder of the Woman's Christian Temperance Union and served elementary, middle, and secondary students.

The 1940s-era Cashmere High School, which stood near the southern end of Division Street, was where the Cashmere School District administrative building is today.

The Cashmere baseball field, pictured here in 1913, once stood on the west side of the mouth of Nahahum Canyon. Cashmere had its own team, as evidenced by articles in the *Cashmere Valley Record*. One can only hope that it won more than it lost.

Shown here is the 1926 annual Fish Feed in Chiwaukum Creek near Lake Wenatchee, approximately 20 miles west of Cashmere. These festivals celebrated the area's abundance of salmon, echoing uncounted generations of Wenatchi who similarly feasted during salmon runs in late summer.

This is a postcard of Matt Hirbay driving a horse and carriage team in the 1905 Cashmere Independence Day parade. Taken near the site of the modern-day Cashmere Museum, the photograph offers a view of Nahahum Canyon in the background. This postcard's back reflects the transition period of the town in 1905. The owner inscribed "Mission" as the location, though the town had been renamed Cashmere the year before.

The Wenatchee Apple Blossom Festival is held in early May each year, and the Liberty Orchards float is a perennial fixture in the procession. This photograph was taken in front of the Cashmere Transfer, close to the modern-day Aplets & Cotlets retail store.

The Cashmere float is shown here on parade at the Wenatchee Apple Blossom Festival around 1950. Cashmere High School's royalty joined all the greater Columbia Basin's delegations in the region's largest festival, held annually in early May since 1919. The only clearly discernible person on the float is Princess Anita at center, but the woman in the rear is likely Queen Judy.

This 1952 parade on Cottage Avenue was most likely celebrating the Fourth of July. In the background is the former three-story Grange and Royal Theater building at the intersection of Cottage Avenue and Woodring Street.

This Liberty Orchards annual Aplets & Cotlets float features future company president Greg Taylor on the left with his relative, Pete Odabashian, on the right, both age seven. Unfortunately, the names of the young woman in the center and the driver to the right of her have both been lost. (Courtesy of Liberty Orchards.)

The aggressive and effective marketing of Aplets & Cotlets is a hallmark of company strategy, and not least among its tools are its annual floats. In this 1934 Wenatchee Apple Blossom Festival photograph, the company employs local youths to advertise its "Confection of the Fairies." (Courtesy of Liberty Orchards.)

Cashmere joined the rest of the Allies in celebrating Japan's surrender to American forces in 1945. During the war, the Ground Observer Corps, an organization affiliated with the Civil Air Patrol, built and manned a lookout station at the top of Olive Street. Conservationists converted the lookout into the Cashmere-Dryden Airport's pilot lounge sometime in the 1950s.

Shown here is the 1943 dedication of the Cashmere lookout station built for the Ground Observer Corps, a military auxiliary organization started during the Second World War. It was located near 221 Olive Street at one of the highest points in town and was in service for seven years, continuing well after the conclusion of World War II, operating 24 hours a day every day of the week. It never saw any hostile aircraft. Later converted into the pilot's lounge at the Cashmere municipal airport, it was nearly delivered to the city dump before Fred Harvey, Cashmere Museum curator, saved it for the museum's collection. From left to right are Ron Doane, unidentified, Elaine Tosch Schmitten, two unidentified, Bill Cox, two unidentified, and Al Adamson.

Orchards in Cashmere were family businesses when they were first planted in the late 1800s. However, by the 1950s, the manual labor market in Cashmere had reached a tipping point away from the children of orchardists, who increasing sought wages higher than what fieldwork could offer. Taking their place were foreign workers who sought the relative economic prosperity offered in the valley's orchards. American government initiatives like the Silva program, likely an outgrowth of the 1942–1964 *bracero*, or manual laborer program, offered contract work to Mexicans. During that period, capital-rich but labor-poor postwar American farms remunerated fieldmen with temporary work visas, pay, a daily food stipend of $1.75, and barracks-style housing, returning them to Mexico when the season was over. Augustine Tovar-Aviña, shown here, was 20 years old in 1957 and netted just $1 per hour for his efforts. (Author's collection.)

This 1976 wedding photograph shows husband Pablo Avila and his bride, Holly Baird. Holly was the daughter of local orchardist Roland "Dick" Baird, who hired Pablo, a bright, moderately bilingual man who entered the United States illegally in 1973 at the age of 20, to serve as his interpreter. Pablo and Holly had a modest honeymoon in the nearby towns of Stehekin and Leavenworth, returning to Cashmere with just enough money to buy that week's groceries. Pablo continues as a field hand today, but has increased his worldly standing and is now landlord to six local rental units. Pablo gained his citizenship in 1986, which he describes as the point when his life turned from that of a Mexican living in America to an American who just happened to be born in Mexico. (Courtesy of Pablo and Holly Avila.)

Pablo Avila, pictured here, came to the United States by means of a coyote, a human trafficker, and crossed the border at Tijuana stuffed into the trunk of a car with three other men. His experience is typical of the hundreds of people who have found a home in Cashmere. Avila recalls emerging in San Diego with no idea where he was, relying entirely on his coyote's promise to deliver him to his friends in California's San Fernando Valley. Avila's parents were Mexican subsistence farmers who had the relative luxury of guaranteeing their own food, but not much else. The house he grew up in was a windowless adobe hut. At the death of his father, when Avila was 16, the family's financial security evaporated, leaving his four younger siblings with no hope of schooling or prosperity. He decided to follow his older brother to the United States in hope of finding work lucrative enough to live and support his family back home. In the background of this December 31, 1976, photograph is the childhood home of Valentine Guzman, Avila's future brother-in-law, who had also traveled to the United States in 1972. (Courtesy of Pablo and Holly Avila.)

Valentine Guzman's parents lived in Mezquital del Oro, Zacatecas, Mexico, under crushing poverty. As a boy, he remembers numerous meals where the only food was one tortilla per person, eaten in a structure of stacked stone with a thatched roof. Ironically, like the Spaniards who colonized Mexico, Guzman hoped to work in the United States only long enough to make enough money to buy a better life for himself and his family back home. Also like many Spaniards, though, marriage to a local cemented him to his new country. The quality of life as a field hand earning just $2 per day was still considerably higher than the starvation conditions of his youth. In this 1974 photograph, Guzman shows the product of his hard work: the fruit that fueled the Cashmere economy. (Courtesy of Valentine Guzman.)

While Mexico may now be well-known for soccer, many of the poor emigrants who streamed across the border into the Cashmere Valley had never once played the sport. In their indigence, even the meager costs of a ball were beyond them. While the new immigrants were constantly fearful of border patrol raids, they were entranced with their newfound ability to afford recreation. The human love of competition prompted them to join local teams. The field hands shown here with their American coach Philip David trained in Peshastin and competed against other teams in central Washington. (Courtesy of Valentine Guzman.)

When Pablo Avila, shown here around 1975, came to America, he entered an island of Mexican culture in a sea of rural America. Upon arrival, immigrants would assume loose group identities based on their work teams, which were usually formed of extended family members. Foremen, often the only ones with vehicles, acted as de facto social leaders and benefactors to their teams. (Courtesy of Pablo and Holly Avila.)

In this c. 2000 photograph, Valentine Guzman sports his *vaquero*, or cowboy, hat in Cashmere. According to Guzman's friend and fellow immigrant Augustine Tovar-Aviña, the moment of gaining citizenship was one of the most profound in his life. In an instant, as Tovar-Aviña describes it, his life changed from one of constant fear and secrecy to one of security and the knowledge that he now belonged where he lived. Those immigrant workers who earn their citizenship begin a new chapter in their families' lives, one that within only a few generations results in children who no more identify with Mexico than other Americans identify with Europe or Africa. (Courtesy of Valentine Guzman.)

Valentine Guzman was nervous when he sat for his first citizenship test in 1985. Wanting to leave his life of illegal residence in the United States behind, he was committed to meeting the requirements of his chosen country. Like many new immigrants, though, he stumbled through his American knowledge test. In 2018, he recalled that his interviewer asked him how many senators there were in Congress and the only answer he could think of was "a lot." Obviously failing that question, he was given one makeup, which was to name the three branches of the US government (the legislative, executive, and judicial). "If I had only known that I had to say those three words!" he later said. Unfortunately, Guzman failed that makeup question too, and was told to study again. On his second attempt several months later, he passed and took the oath of citizenship in Yakima on March 5, 1985. (Courtesy of Valentine Guzman.)

Valentine Guzman and Lauren "Lochlyn" Baird were married on November 18, 1978. He was an immigrant fruit picker and she was the daughter of a local orchardist (and sister to the aforementioned Holly Baird). Early in their marriage, Valentine and Lochlyn lived happily but humbly in Mexico. Guzman recounts that when they were raising their young family, his wife would wash their children's cloth diapers in a creek, being unable to afford washing machines or even a trip to the laundromat. Yet, upon their return to Cashmere, Guzman said that his life grew "always better and better." He felt comfortable in his new country, learning the language well enough to interpret, and raising children in the local Cashmere School District. "I don't feel like I am a stranger here," he said at the age of 68. "I have friends everywhere." He earned these friendships through the hard work he invested in his community, including his retirement job of school bus driver, and the loyalty he showed to those friends and family he was able to endow with financial security. (Courtesy of Valentine Guzman.)

360 Self Rd.
Cashmere, WA 98815-958
September 26, 2011

Mr. Guzman
5970 Sunburst Lane
Cashmere, WA 98815-958

Dear Mr. Guzman

Thank you for waking up in the morning every day to take us to school when our parents were working. And get us to school on time every day. When it is Halloween or any other holiday you give us candy and wish us a great weekend. You make sure everyone is happy with their seats like the high school section and middle school and then vale.

You are a nice bus driver but can be strict and make sure everyone is being good. You make sure that everyone is sitting property because if you happen to brake everyone is safe and **doesn't get hurt. You make sure that nobody is eating gum because if you hit a bump then they won't choke.** You drive in a slow safe rate to get us a school.

I just want to say thank you for all the nice things you do for us every day. And when I was the **student of the bus and I got to go to Brian's pizza. Thank you for choosing me for that. Have a nice day.** ☺

Sincerely

Bianca Gomez

Bianca Gomez
Bus Rider

Bianca Gomez	September 26, 2011	Letter 4

According to Valentine Guzman (who in 2011 was in his 39th year in Cashmere and his 26th as a citizen), this letter exemplifies what he and many other Mexicans, illegal and otherwise, hope to achieve: a truly positive impact on their community, their places of worship, and their adopted home. Bianca Gomez was likely a freshman in high school when she wrote this letter, which resulted in Cashmere School District superintendent Glenn Johnson giving Guzman a letter of commendation. (Courtesy of Valentine Guzman.)

Picking pears is a task that requires great physical endurance. Orchard workers move ladders and picking bags, which are carried on the chest, from tree to tree. Pear stems have a natural curve to them, and pickers raise the fruit against the curve to snap it off at the branch. They then place the fragile pears into their bags, which when full are gently emptied into wooden fruit bins. Foremen then move these bins by tractor, keeping pace with their crews. The work can be hazardous; Augustine Tovar-Aviña recounts several of his less adroit coworkers tumbling off their ladders. In 2018, Tovar-Aviña proudly said that he had never fallen from a ladder, but he did admit to several close calls when he saved himself only by clinging in terror to a rough pear branch. (Courtesy of Valentine Guzman.)

New immigrant workers occasionally had private or semiprivate kitchens where they could cook for themselves, like the one shown here, but they more often ate at field kitchens that foremen or contracting companies provided. When asked for his most memorable food experience upon arriving in the United States, Augustine Tovar-Aviña remembers a field lunch where his cooks made fresh tortillas. They did not have the proper cooking tools, and he was disgusted when one baker continually licked his fingertips to keep them from burning as he handled the tortillas. However, as revolting as he found that to be, Tovar-Aviña, 81, said with a smile that he heartily ate every tortilla he could get his hands on. (Courtesy of Valentine Guzman.)

Many of the apples, pears, and cherries that men like Augustine Tovar-Aviña and Valentine Guzman picked end up here, at the Crunch Pak factory complex. Originally the JA Prentis Cold Storage Warehouse from 1907 to 1929, the buildings that made up the warehouse compound also housed the Northwestern Fruit Exchange and the Dow Fruit Company from 1910 to 1922, as well as the Trunkey-Wolfe & Company fruit brokers in 1925. The facility went through several more ownerships, including that of the WenYak Fruit Company of the mid-1930s (owned by Cashmere Museum patron Willis Carey and his associate Melvin Babcock) until 1940, when it became the Cashmere Fruit Exchange. In 2000, the Crunch Pak Company bought the facilities and used them to develop an innovative and simple method of slicing, washing, and preserving fresh fruit in single-serving bags. These small helpings of fruit now have international reach as part of McDonald's Happy Meals. (Courtesy of the *Spokesman Review* and Crunch Pak.)

This undated aerial photograph shows the beautiful Vale of Cashmere looking southwest. Clearly visible at top are the eastern slopes of the Cascade Range and the prominent Highway 2. Local traffic is still dominated by the railway, generally running along the south side of the river, with frequent freight and passenger trains passing through downtown. At upper left is Mission Creek, whose waters mix with those of Brender Creek at center, until they reach the swift Wenatchee River. (Author's collection.)

Afterword

Ever held a piece of embroidery in your hands? The front is regular, neat, and orderly, organized into a clear and distinct pattern. This is the history you read. Now, flip that tapestry over. On its back you will recognize something like the front's pattern—but the edges are frayed, and the image is rough, and the threads often connect in seemingly contradictory ways. This is what real history, how we actually live, is like. The order and logic of books like *Cashmere* are the result of the imposition of time, effort, and skill, the things necessary to assemble history's stitches into sense.

The Roman chronicler Tacitus once said that "all translations of . . . importance are wrapt in doubt and obscurity." Overcoming that doubt and obscurity is our challenge in the 21st century, just like it was his in the 1st. Primary source material—photographs, interviews, and handwritten letters on paper that need to be smoothed out just to be read—make up the back of the tapestry that is the human experience. The exhaustive process of weaving these records together is, as Tacitus tells us, inherently flawed. If those who lived those times did not fully understand them (and they didn't), how much can we? Yet, a researcher can begin to assemble anecdotes and artifacts into a pattern, a story from which we can draw meaning. That is what this and every other history is: a collection of firsthand stories, personal treasures, and the accumulated knowledge of those who have devoted their lives to preserving our memories.

This book is a small example of this, a tapestry of all the threads that make up our town and its place in the wider world. Even more than this, though, it is a labor of love. The stories that emerge from the research are as much a eulogy of those who came before us as they are a record of them. It is incomplete, as is all history, as is all human understanding, yet it is still vitally important because it is part of who we are—and how we will live is the product of who we once were.

—Alexandra R. Palmer-Gapper
Director, Cashmere Museum and Pioneer Village
December 21, 2018
Cashmere, Washington

BIBLIOGRAPHY

Arksey, Laura. "Cashmere – Thumbnail History." Historylink.org. Last modified August 30, 2008. Accessed April 25, 2018. http://historylink.org/File/8750.

Brender, Lance B. *23 Moses-Columbia Verbs*. Charleston, SC: CreateSpace, 2018.

Brooks, Ernest K'saw's. "Learned Something." E-mail, 2018.

Brouillette, Joseph F.X., interview by author, Cashmere, WA, 2016–2018.

Clark, Ella E. *Indian Legends of the Pacific Northwest*. Berkeley, CA: University of California Press, 1953.

Czaykowska-Higgins, Ewa, and M. Dale Kinkade, editors. *Salish Languages and Linguistics: Theoretical and Descriptive Perspectives*. New York, NY: Mouton de Gruyter, 1998.

Dow, Edson. *Passes to the North: History of the Wenatchee Mountains*. Wenatchee, WA: Wenatchee Bindery and Printing Company: 1963.

Ethnologue. "Columbia-Wenatchi." Accessed June 12, 2018. https://www.ethnologue.com/language/col.

Garcia, Jerry. *Mexicans in North Central Washington*. Charleston, SC: Arcadia Publishing, 2007.

Hall, Sharon Graves. *Tiny: King of the Roadside Vendors*. Snohomish, WA: Cloudcap, 1991.

Harvey, Fred, interview by author, Cashmere, WA, 2016–2018.

Ingraham, Linda. *1904–2004 Cashmere History: Old Photos & Newspaper Clippings*. Unpublished.

Johnson, Dorene. *Cottage Avenue*. Fuzz Publishing, 2014.

Keyser, James D. *Indian Rock Art of the Columbia Plateau*. Seattle, WA: University of Washington Press, 1997.

Kinney-Holck, Rose, and The Upper Valley Museum at Leavenworth. *Leavenworth*. Charleston, SC: Arcadia Publishing, 2008.

Krist, Gary. *The White Cascade: The Great Northern Railway Disaster and America's Deadliest Avalanche*. New York, NY: Henry Holt & Company, 2007.

Lane, George. *Making Wawa: The Genesis of Chinook Jargon*. Vancouver, BC: University of British Columbia Press, 2008.

Palmer, Lexie, interview by author, Cashmere, WA, 2016–2018.

Scheuerman, Richard D., editor. *The Wenatchi Indians: Guardians of the Valley*. Fairfield, WA: Ye Galleon Press: 1982.

———. *The Wenatchee Valley: And its First Peoples*. Walla Walla, WA: Color Press, 2005.

Shutler, Nolan. "Taking the Bitter with the Sweet: Wenatchee Fishing Rights." Lewis & Clark College. Last modified July 31, 2011. Accessed June 11, 2018. http://law.lclark.edu/live/files/9435-13tojcishutlerpdf.

Trafzer, Clifford E., editor. *Grandmother, Grandfather, and Old Wolf: Tamánwit Ku Súkat and Traditional Native American Narratives from the Columbia Plateau*. East Lansing, MI: Michigan State University Press, 2008.

USA Basketball. "Hailey Van Lith." Last modified October 26, 2018. Accessed January 6, 2019. www.usab.com/basketball/players/womens/v/van-lith-hailey.aspx

Wenatchee Valley Museum and Cultural Center, Chris Rader, and Mark Behler. *Wenatchee*. Charleston, SC: Arcadia Publishing, 2012.

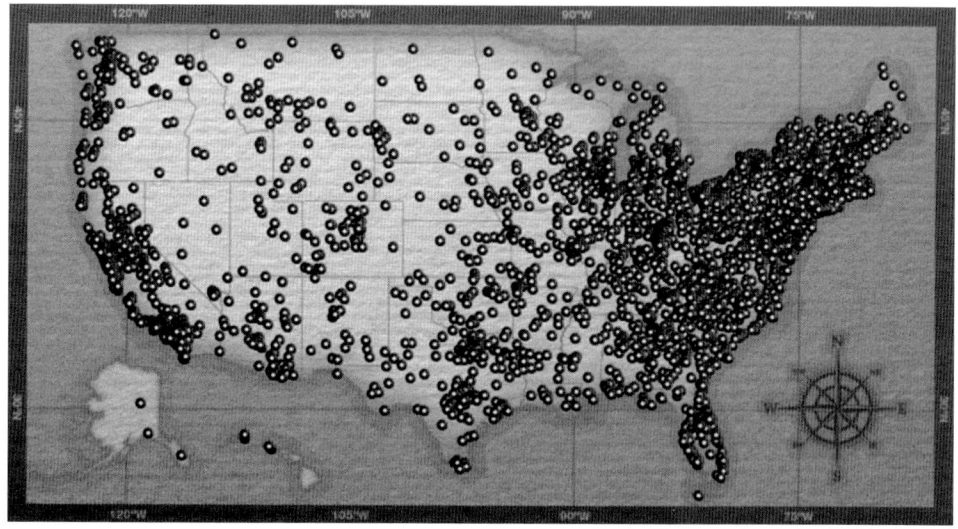